Rapid Organizational Change

Rapid Organizational Change

STEVEN BLEISTEIN

WILEY

This edition first published 2017
© 2017 John Wiley & Sons, Ltd

Registered office
John Wiley & Sons Ltd, The Atrium, Southern Gate, Chichester, West Sussex, PO19 8SQ,
United Kingdom

For details of our global editorial offices, for customer services and for information about
how to apply for permission to reuse the copyright material in this book please see our
website at www.wiley.com.

Wiley publishes in a variety of print and electronic formats and by print-on-demand.
Some material included with standard print versions of this book may not be included
in e-books or in print-on-demand. If this book refers to media such as a CD or DVD that
is not included in the version you purchased, you may download this material at http://
booksupport.wiley.com. For more information about Wiley products, visit www.wiley.com.

Designations used by companies to distinguish their products are often claimed as
trademarks. All brand names and product names used in this book are trade names,
service marks, trademarks or registered trademarks of their respective owners. The
publisher is not associated with any product or vendor mentioned in this book.

Limit of Liability/Disclaimer of Warranty: While the publisher and author have used their
best efforts in preparing this book, they make no representations or warranties with
respect to the accuracy or completeness of the contents of this book and specifically
disclaim any implied warranties of merchantability or fitness for a particular purpose. It
is sold on the understanding that the publisher is not engaged in rendering professional
services and neither the publisher nor the author shall be liable for damages arising
herefrom. If professional advice or other expert assistance is required, the services of a
competent professional should be sought.

Library of Congress Cataloging-in-Publication Data is Available:

ISBN 978-1-119-21903-3 (hardback) ISBN 978-1-119-21904-0 (ePub)
ISBN 978-1-119-21905-7 (ePDF)

Cover Design: Wiley
Cover Image: © ulimi/Getty Images, Inc.

Set in 10/12 ITC Garamond Std by SPi Global, Chennai, India

Printed in Great Britain by TJ International Ltd, Padstow, Cornwall, UK

10 9 8 7 6 5 4 3 2 1

Contents

Preface

S ince I was a teenager growing up in Denver, Colorado in the United States, I have had a love for foreign language and a fascination with other countries and people throughout the world. That fascination has taken me around the world, starting with France, where I did a year-long study abroad at a high school in Lyon during my junior year.

In all the places I have lived, studied, worked, and done business, I have noticed that people are far more similar than dissimilar, particularly at a deeper level beyond the superficial behaviors that one can observe and call "culture."

Culture in my view is nothing more than an alternative manifestation of the values we all share as human beings. Cultural difference need not matter if you can address the values rather than their manifestations. Much of my business is helping leaders do just that, whether in Japan or France, or elsewhere, regardless of the nationalities of the people whom the leader leads.

The goal of this book is to share some of that wisdom with you, so you can achieve the same success that I have enabled others to achieve. In my experience, there is nothing stopping you or anyone else.

Steven Bleistein
Tokyo, Japan

Acknowledgments

I would like to thank my many clients who have been an extraordinary source of inspiration and learning for me, and Dr Alan Weiss, my personal mentor, for all his help and advice in making this book a reality.

I dedicate this book to Professor Norman Bleistein, my father and world famous geophysicist, who always saw what is possible and not just what is; to my mother Sandra Bleistein, who always inspired the best in everyone; and to my son Alexandre, my mother's namesake, who takes after her in ways he cannot know. Finally, I would like to thank my wife, the love of my life, who makes all my success possible.

About the Author

Dr Steven Jeffrey Bleistein is the founder and CEO of Relansa Inc., and is one of those rare international experts who bridges Western and Japanese business thinking. Fluent in Japanese and French, Steve has attracted clients from businesses such as Adidas Japan, Lenovo Japan, Reckitt Benckiser, Nikko Chemicals, NTT Data Group, and Mitsubishi Bank. Working with leaders and their teams, Steve helps both Japanese and international companies create their own new realities. Prior to Relansa, Steve represented the Balanced Scorecard Institute in Japan. Steve serves as Vice Chair of the Independent Business Committee of the American Chamber of Commerce in Japan, where he takes an active role in supporting entrepreneurial and leadership capabilities inside Japanese companies. He runs the popular "Conversation With" luncheon series, where he leads an on-stage conversation with a local business leader guest. In addition, Steve serves on the board of Tsukuba International School, supporting the school's leadership on the path toward full International Baccalaureate certification. Prior to returning to Japan in 2009, Steve drove innovation on a multimillion dollar project at Australia's premier government IT innovation think-tank NICTA, forging collaborative relationships with Japanese IT giants. In addition, Steve assisted Japan's Cabinet Office on issues related to e-government strategy, and organized joint meetings between the Japanese Government and Australian Commonwealth officials.

Rapid Organizational Change

CHAPTER 1

The Refraction Layer

M any CEOs of companies complain of resistance to change in their organizations. The problem of resistance to change appears to be particularly acute in Japan. In fact, many CEOs of companies in Japan lament that the Japanese are the most resistant to organizational change of any people in the world. I often hear this even from business leaders who are Japanese themselves!

Most CEOs have been able to build a leadership team around them whose members are change-oriented and like-minded in thinking. Sometimes that team extends to one or two layers of management below. Yet, it is frequently the rest of the organization that is viewed as remaining stubbornly recalcitrant. But is it really?

What is Refraction Anyway?

My father is one of the world's foremost experts on wave phenomena. A brilliant mathematician who found his calling in the field of geophysics, he developed methods for imaging the interior of the Earth using sound waves propagated from the surface. I remember seeing printouts on the walls of my father's study, showing the different geological layers deep in the interior of the Earth—where there is hard rock, soft rock, water, and even oil! Other printouts showed how the different layers bend, reflect, and dampen the sound waves.

It is the difference in substance from one layer to the next that alters the waves when they pass from a layer of one substance to another. A wave may be bent, and change direction. Or it may be partially deflected back up to the surface, with a weakened wave continuing downward. Some waves dissipate entirely. So the waves that reach deeper into the Earth are really distortions of the ones that came from the surface, perhaps weakened, if they reach the deeper layers at all. In the physical world, the bending of waves is called *refraction*.

The layers of management and staff within a company are not unlike the geological layers of the Earth, and *refraction* occurs in companies as well. However, it is not a difference in physical substance that refracts waves of change, but rather a difference in thinking at different levels of management. The waves of change a leader attempts to propagate down through the company behave much like sound waves propagating down through the layers of the Earth. They may

FIGURE 1.1 Deflecting, refracting, and dissipating waves of change

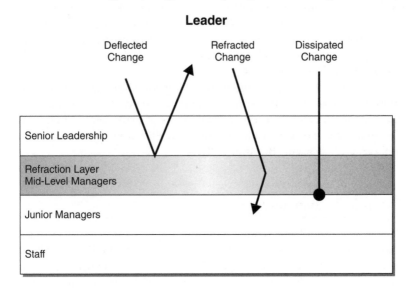

bend and change direction, be partially deflected, or dissipate entirely. So the waves of change that reach deeper levels of the company become distortions of the change that a leader had intended, and sometimes never reach the deeper levels at all. See Figure 1.1.

In geophysics, interpreting the feedback of sound waves at the surface is a technically difficult problem, because refraction layers deep in the Earth mask what is below and alter waves that return to the surface. In companies, it can be just as tricky for a leader to interpret the feedback returning to the top, because refraction layers in management frequently mask what transpires below. From the top, it can look as if the entire organization is resistant to change. However, I have found that what can, at first glance, appear as widespread recalcitrance in the organization, is rarely actually the case. On the contrary, more often than not, most managers and staff are open to change.

In my experience, what may appear to be widespread resistance to change is in fact limited to a *refraction layer* of mid-level managers. Resolve the issues with the refraction layer first, and the organization beneath is freed to change. Leave the refraction layer intact and, no matter how forceful your attempts to promote change, it is very likely that they will inevitably fail. The mistake that most leaders make is rolling out change to the company as a whole once the leadership team is aligned and on-board, taking much time, effort, and energy, without first paying heed to refraction layers. Without addressing refraction layers first, the great energy and time spent on complex change efforts is squandered.

The problem is that most approaches to change treat a company as an entity of uniform substance, whereas an organization is more akin to the diversity of substance in geology. Typical approaches to organizational change tend to be elaborate and multi-staged. We have become accustomed to change being a long, hard process, fraught with risk of failure, because this is what we have been told and what we have experienced. However, it does not need to be that way.

I have never met a CEO who talked about change as something less than an urgent priority. By identifying and eliminating refraction layers first, leaders can achieve change in their organizations with maximum speed and efficiency of effort, and dramatically increase likelihood of sustainability and success. This book provides not only tools for doing so, but also methods and processes to help ensure refraction layers do not develop in the first place.

Leadership Proximity Trumps Leadership Rank

Leadership starts at the top but lives or dies in the middle. Staff take their cues from their immediate managers, no matter what a CEO might proclaim or communicate from their lofty perch. After all, it is their immediate managers whom they must serve every day, who evaluate their performance, who hold sway over their remuneration and promotion, and who can make a workday exciting, uneventful, or otherwise an unbearable form of hell. While staff may be open to the change the CEO desires, they will tend to behave in accordance with the priorities of their immediate manager, or at least avoid behaving in a way that they might oppose.

All it takes is one recalcitrant mid-level manager to block movement toward change of everyone down their reporting line. That can be a huge swath of the organization, depending on the level of the mid-level manager, and how flat the organization is. The more levels of staff below the manager, the deeper the impact. The flatter the organization, the wider the impact. A recalcitrant manager is like an object blocking a source of

FIGURE 1.2 Principle of projection

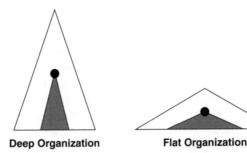

Deep Organization   **Flat Organization**

light waves. The shadow cast depends on the proximity of the object to the source. In this case, the source is the leader and the light is waves of change. I call this the principle of projection. See Figure 1.2.

Change simply does not work its way from the bottom up. The greatest mistake I see leaders make is focusing efforts on the more junior managers and staff when it is more senior-level ones that hold sway. I have seen many companies go to great lengths to communicate new direction, new methods, and new thinking throughout the organization down to junior staff, seeking "buy-in"—all of which is wasted because a handful of mid-level managers simply don't buy-in. CEO roadshows to explain the changes, the need for change, and the merits for changing are all for naught. Training and orientation workshops will have little effect. Even revised performance evaluation schemes will not be effective when it is the immediate manager who conducts the review. None of these tools are effective among staff and managers whose immediate manager is not on-board.

Layers of Sedimentary Rock

Several managers at the same middle level who have relatively uniform thinking in resisting change form a layer of sedimentary rock within the organization that will block change for all layers below. When a group of managers think in a similar way, they reinforce each other's certainty in the correctness of their point of view, making the refraction layer only that much more difficult to penetrate.

Why do these layers of sedimentary rock form in the first place? I have often heard leaders lay the blame of recalcitrance at the feet of the mid-level managers themselves. While individual recalcitrance is certainly an individual's choice, the causes of formation of refraction layers often lie with choices a *leader* may make, not with the mid-level managers. Below are four such causes over which a leader has direct control.

Overprotection of labor—by choice!

In many countries, including Japan, there are strong protective labor laws and regulations. It is convenient to blame government for the results of overprotecting labor. Government regulation is more often an excuse for leaders to avoid the sometimes uncomfortable task of removing non-performing managers, rather than an actual impediment.

CEOs in Japan, whether Japanese or foreign, often tell me that it is "illegal" to fire anyone in Japan. Yet, this is definitely not the case. Termination in Japan is a matter of procedure, time, and money—like everywhere else in the world, no matter how strict or liberal the labor laws. Even in countries like France, which has highly protective labor laws, it is possible to remove non-performers, although it may require a longer process or cost more to do so than in countries with less restrictive laws.

When a Japanese CEO tells me that firing is illegal, I believe it is partly because of the tradition of lifetime employment from which they may come. Firing is distasteful for most people anywhere in the world, but particularly distasteful in Japan where employment for many had once been for life. In Japan, firing is viewed almost as an end-of-the-world level calamity by many. There is a gravity to firing in Japan that does not exist elsewhere. The legal justification merely makes it easier to avoid confronting the uncomfortable idea that the business may be better off without someone—and perhaps the employee will be better off as well!

When I ask a foreign CEO what makes them think firing someone is illegal, the typical response is, "My Japanese HR director told me so!" I believe many Japanese HR directors are loath to deal with terminations for many of the same reasons as Japanese CEOs, and exaggerate the difficulties and risks of doing so, particularly to their non-Japanese bosses.

As such, non-performers and even destructive employees are often left in place, promoted, or transferred laterally so they become someone else's problem. Or in the case of Japan, they become part of "windowsill gangs"—non-performing managers who are simply sidelined and given limited responsibility—and a metaphorical desk by the window so they can look outside and not become completely bored as they whittle the time away during a business day. However, these practices create layer upon layer of sedimentary rock within an organization and buttress refraction.

For example, an executive client of mine had actually proposed taking a non-performing manager and promoting him to a position of head of strategic planning inside the company, the rationale being that the strategic planning group was not that important or influential (a view which, you will certainly agree, is an issue in itself!). However, the non-performing manager would still have staff in the strategic planning group, some of whom were young, talented, and enthusiastic, and had potential to create a lot of value for the company. Any zeal for growth, ambitious targets, and excitement at the prospect of change emanating from above would never reach this group under that manager. And it gets worse ... I pointed out to the executive how the staff under the non-performing manager would wither. Their skills would atrophy. They would become demoralized and cynical. They would fail to grow and achieve their full potential, and might even leave the company! The company would be far better off paying the non-performing manager to retire early and building up a productive strategic planning team, rather than condemn a group of potential next generation leaders to mediocrity or even possibly losing them to competitors! Financially alone, the business would be better off, not to mention the enthusiasm and emotional well-being of the staff!

Keeping non-performers creates refraction layers, even when the non-performers are sidelined. Whatever the cause, overprotection of labor—beyond what is practical, fair, or required for regulatory compliance reasons—forms refraction layers.

Seniority-Based Promotion

Similar to overprotection of labor is seniority-based promotion. During the postwar era, seniority-based promotion, as opposed to performance-based promotion, was standard practice in most companies. Today, it is not uncommon for the leaders of Japanese companies to claim that their seniority-based promotion system has been replaced with a meritocracy. However, in many companies, the meritocracy is more aspirational than actual, and seniority-based promotion continues in practice if not in policy—even in foreign companies in Japan!

In one such company, I suggested to the CEO to promote a top-performing sales manager to a senior-level role. Despite agreeing that the candidate would be a top performer and create a lot of value for the company, he responded, "I could not possibly promote him! He would have subordinates who are older than he is! Think of how they would feel!"

My retort was, "Think of how your star performers will feel when you give priority to the fragile feelings of mediocre managers over business results! Your mediocre managers, even if their feelings are hurt, will stay with your company, but do you think your star performer will remain with you if his results are not rewarded?"

Seniority-based promotion and lifetime employment may have been the pillars of Japanese corporate life for many years, but these practices are not unique to Japan. Other companies around the world have tended to reward years of service for promotion over performance. No matter where a business is in the world, any system that blocks the flow of innovative management talent creates refraction layers. Yet seniority-based promotion is one of the most insidious causes of refraction layers, as it deliberately creates layers of calcified rock in a company, with uniform advancement based on years of service or age. In the end, it is the leader who decides how talent moves or does not move inside the company. An effective leader can scrap the system, or at least limit its extent within the organization by paying close attention to promotions one or two levels directly below him. Many leaders still fail to appreciate how toxic seniority-based promotion can be and lack the resolve to change the status quo.

Leadership Fear of Staff

Leadership fear of staff is surprisingly common, particularly in foreign companies in Japan. It usually occurs between senior-level sales directors and executive management. An executive, particularly an expat executive, is often afraid to push a veteran Japanese sales director too hard on change in sales strategy because they fear damaging or losing key customer relationships that a sales director supposedly owns. Instead, the executive turns their attention to retraining sales staff, which is utterly useless while the sales director is still in power, because as mentioned previously, leadership proximity trumps leadership rank.

Many mid-level managers are aware of this power over their superiors—and some use it! In one the most brazen cases I have encountered, the CEO of a major foreign brand here told me how his head of sales deliberately implemented his own idea of strategy with a key account, doing the opposite of the decisions made with the CEO. When confronted by the CEO after the fact, the sales director threatened to resign. The CEO backed down for fear of losing the key customer account altogether.

The CEO later asked me what he should do. My advice was to fire the sales director, and he did. His Japanese HR director put up a fight—told him this was illegal (it was not), and even contacted the head of global HR in New York to try to rally support and get her boss to back down. In the end, the CEO did not back down, and the head of sales lost his job. The result? The company had a record year for growth, outpacing every other market where the brand is present.

The company did not lose a single key account, as the CEO had feared. The customers were making far too much money from the business relationship to be derailed by a personal spat! However, other leaders in similar cases have allowed such senior staff to remain out of fear, effectively creating a refraction layer themselves. Every person, leader or not, has control over his own fear, and should never be driven by fear when making decisions!

Rewarding Lack of Failure as Success

Growth-oriented people view failure as learning, and as such are the most open to change. I once had the following discussion with the HR director of a major IT product business in Japan:

ME	Say you have two candidates for a position, both equal in experience, education, and skill. You ask both the same question in an interview. "Tell me about a time that you failed at something important." One responds, "I have never failed at anything." The other responds, "Just one failure? I have failed at many important things. What kind of failure would you like to hear about?" Who would you hire?
HR DIRECTOR	The one who had never failed, of course!

It is impossible to succeed at anything without failure. People who cannot deal with failure won't learn. Those who won't learn, won't change or grow. They will postpone actions and decisions for fear of ruining their spotless records. They will wait for others to act, because the safest route to avoid responsibility for failure is to avoid responsibility altogether.

A culture that rewards lack of failure as success, whether explicitly or tacitly, creates refraction layers at all levels. Let me be clear here. I am not proposing that a leader should reward failure due to lack of competence or negligence. Nor am I suggesting that recklessness should be rewarded. In order to succeed in business, a manager must take on reasonable risk. Some endeavors will naturally fail. If failure is always penalized, even for a good idea that just did not work, managers will avoid taking on reasonable risk. Avoiding reasonable risk is in effect a highly risky behavior, as the business is bound to fail. The behavior of taking on reasonable risk is far more important to the success of the business than single successes or failures.

A leader has control over which behavior is rewarded and which is not. Reward behaviors, not just results. Give people permission to fail. Penalize inaction. Take control over reward criteria, rather than leaving it entirely to HR.

Any organization that penalizes failure when managers take on reasonable risk will naturally create a whole class of mid-level leaders who avoid any type of risk. Change has inherent risk and, as such, a leader will have inadvertently created a refraction layer of mid-level managers who will oppose change of any type.

A leader should not underestimate their own power to keep refraction layers from forming in the first place—or of their susceptibility to a refractive organization, should they allow it.

Dearth of Leadership Bench

An organization that is full of refraction layers typically also suffers from leadership dearth as the former begets the latter. A growing and changing organization has constant appetite for new leaders at all levels that must be satiated, and the fastest way to achieve that is from a pool of internal candidates. CEOs, however, often tell me how their pool is inadequate or otherwise non-existent, this despite a plethora of people with the right titles and requisite years of experience! CEOs have complained to me how they feel that they have often had to compromise—placing a candidate who was not right for the role simply because no one else was available immediately, and there was no time to field external candidates, let alone allow an external hire process the time to ramp up to hire someone who was best-in-class.

When a mid-level manager opposes the thinking and strategic direction of the firm, and decides to resist it, whether actively or passively, they prevent change from above reaching their staff. They will be overly worried about risk related to the new and the different, and as such often turn out to be a poor candidate for a more senior position where the ability to respond to change is critical. If many managers think similarly and decide to resist in the same way, then the pool of candidates narrows further. Because of the principle of proximity of leadership, the thinking and associated behaviors are projected below, leading to a dearth of leadership bench at more junior levels as well. The organization overall experiences a dearth of leadership bench at all levels, including for junior positions, not just senior ones. Attempting to develop more staff to become leaders is bound to fail because the reason for the dearth of leadership bench is not lack of talent, but rather a refraction layer above them.

For example, I coached four talented sales team leaders in an organization, each of whom had different sales directors, three of whom formed a refraction layer, and the fourth who was a top performer. All the team leaders had talent and enthusiastically absorbed learning and began to change behavior and improved performance while I was actively coaching them. However, the team leaders under the refraction layer directors quickly reverted to old ways, and dropped to previous performance levels after the end of my engagement. They simply could not spread their wings under their bosses. The fourth team leader, however, did sustain improvement and continued to improve performance under his boss, also a top performer. That team leader was promoted to an international director position himself not long after.

The other three managers were ultimately transferred and placed under the management of the fourth director. As soon as they were, performance improved. However, time was lost just when the company was in need of good mid-level leaders. They are all on their way to a promotion, but their fourth colleague made director at least two years ahead of the time when they will first become eligible to do so.

Allowing refraction layers to build up in an organization not only causes it to calcify, but leaves it perpetually without a sufficient mid-level leadership bench. Junior staff skills are hampered and their career paths are handicapped as well, creating a permanent state of lack of depth to the leadership bench, both in the present and into the future.

Eliminating Refraction

What causes refraction layers? Is it the fault of local culture, Japanese or otherwise? Is it the fault of the local education system? Is it the fault of the managers themselves, who perhaps never should have been hired in the first place? I have heard CEOs cite all these causes and more, and to some degree they may be right. However, none of these are the root cause.

Do you lead an organization as I do and have done? If so, I have some good news and some bad news. First the bad news: the root cause of refraction in your organization may be, well, us. As leaders we may inadvertently create refraction or otherwise unwittingly allow refraction to persist. The good news is that we, as leaders, have the power not only to eliminate refraction in our organizations, but also to keep refraction from recurring in the future, clearing a path for rapid change. How, you ask?

We start by changing our thinking. We follow through by changing current practices to eliminate refraction in current business, and strengthening or starting practices that keep new refraction layers from forming in the future.

As such, I have organized this book into three parts:

1. Eliminating refraction from thinking: In this part, I bust the Galapagos myth—the idea that somehow Japan is unique and so practices that work elsewhere in the world do not apply in Japan. The equivalent of the Galapagos myth outside of Japan is the leader who insists, "We're different!" I not only bust the Galapagos myth, but also provide insights that help break through Galapagos thinking. I then describe what a growth- and change-oriented manager looks like compared to those who are not, so that you can recognize them. Without stopping there, I provide ways of changing thinking among mid-level managers to eliminate refraction.

2. Eliminating refraction in the current business: This refraction includes practices such as traditional hiring, overprotection of labor, obsessive focus on hard work at the expense of achieving results, and clear methods for closing performance gaps.
3. Preventing refraction from recurring: In this final part, I detail practices for maximizing speed of growth and change, hiring right, and cultivating a perpetual leadership bench.

Japan as a Crucible

Many of the examples in this book come from Japan, but do not let that put you off just because you don't happen to work in Japan. Refraction layers are not unique to Japanese companies. I have done business in the United States, France, Australia, Hong Kong, and Japan. The refraction layer phenomenon exists in companies in all these countries and in others around the world. However, refraction layers are a particularly acute problem in Japanese companies, which makes case studies from that market ideal to illustrate both problems and potential solutions.

Many foreign companies in Japan—like Adidas, Nike, Godiva, Lenovo, Unilever—use Japan as a crucible for new products and methods because the market and consumer demands in Japan are so high. If you can succeed with a product in Japan, you can succeed anywhere.

Japan has served as a crucible for the methods described in this book. You can also find additional resources at *www.relansa.co.jp*. Those methods can be applied anywhere with equal success. If you can achieve change in a Japanese company, you can achieve change in any company anywhere. So, let's get started!

The Myth of Uniqueness

A s leaders, we are sometimes our own worst enemies when it comes to creating refraction layers or allowing them to persist as a result of mistaken assumptions, based on which we make decisions for action, or in many cases inaction. In Japan, the most frequent refraction-layer-generating, mistaken assumption I encounter centers around so-called "uniqueness" of the Japanese. And for that matter, I have heard the same often of Americans, English, Germans, French, Australians, Singaporeans, Chinese Koreans, and the people of countries around the world about which similar assertions can be, and often are, made. However, it is has been my experience that people are far more similar than dissimilar where it counts, and uniqueness is more often an excuse for, rather than a cause of, failure to change.

Many CEOs I meet, whether Japanese or not, assume that the Japanese are somehow unique among humans. I frequently hear CEOs say that the problem is Japanese culture, and that the Japanese are somehow so different that methods used in other countries simply don't work here. Some CEOs claim they are helpless in the face of resistance to change among mid-level managers due to the national culture of Japan. However, this is simply not the case. Yet when they encounter a problem in changing the business in some way, as all senior leaders inevitably do, Japanese culture often becomes a rationalization for the failure to effectively implement the change, an excuse not to act, or not to act on their own business instincts as they would do in other countries.

While differences in behavior and attitude from one country to another exist, I challenge the idea that Japanese people are somehow an exception to the rule when it comes to changing culture in organizations. In this regard, the Japanese are motivated in the same ways as other members of the entire human race. CEOs have enormous power to set the culture of their organizations, and an organization's culture has far greater bearing on behavior than national culture. If you can understand the fundamentals of what drives people, you can lead people to change, even in Japan.

Busting the Galapagos Myth

Japan is often referred to as a *Galapagos*. The reference to the Galapagos, the islands made famous by Charles Darwin, is of course a metaphor. The reasoning goes that because Japan is/has been cut off from the rest of the world, it has given rise to a unique people with a unique way of doing things. What works elsewhere cannot possibly work in Japan. What is taken as given elsewhere, does not apply to Japan. As such, Japan has often been referred to as enigmatic, impenetrable to non-Japanese, and a black box for international companies. In my view, these ideas are exaggerated, if not completely unfounded, and nothing more than what is unfortunately a widely accepted myth about Japan and the Japanese.

If you find the Japanese mysterious, that is because of your prejudice, and is not down to the Japanese. The Japanese are neither enigmatic nor different from the rest of the human race to such an extent that what applies elsewhere does not apply in Japan. Just because something may not make sense at first glance, does not mean it cannot be understood. If you were to witness inexplicable behavior in any country other than Japan, you would not immediately conclude that understanding the people in that country is impossible, or requires some kind of special gift of zen-like insight. You would simply think that you don't yet understand a cultural quirk. And, assuming that you are a curious person, you will want to find out and learn about it.

So why is there this mystique around Japan? I believe part of the reason is because many people buy into the myth simply because it is easier to do so than the hard work of learning about a foreign country, or the resolve that is required to insist on change. They choose to be persuaded by those around them. And it is not only outsiders who buy into Japan and the Japanese being special and unfathomable. Many Japanese themselves believe that as a people, understanding them is impossible for outsiders. Many Japanese love to point out how unique they are as a people and a country, how different Japan is from every foreign country and how different they are from the people who come from those countries.

However, this often is used as an excuse for not wanting to change—for example, not wanting to learn English, not wanting to adopt a new way of selling to customers, not wanting to change a product line-up, not wanting to try an alternative method of distribution, not wanting to implement a merit-based promotion system, not wanting to eliminate overtime in a Japanese company, not wanting to put women in real positions in management, etc. The list goes on and on.

"We cannot do this because this is Japan and we are Japanese!" becomes the perfect ironclad excuse for not changing. After all, you cannot single-handedly expect to change Japanese culture or Japanese history, or simply change the fact that someone is Japanese. Because so many Japanese believe that Japan and the Japanese are unique, the excuse is often accepted *a priori* without question—and many company leaders, both Japanese and non-Japanese, buy into the excuse as well.

The Galapagos myth is one of the greatest impediments to change in a Japanese company, and it is self-imposed, because it patently does not reflect reality. People will argue with you about the immutability of Japanese companies because of the nature of Japanese culture. They will point at examples of large Japanese companies with "traditional" ways of doing business that resist all attempts at reform. Without a doubt, and without naming some of the more infamous ones, these companies do exist. However, they are not the standard bearer for every other company in Japan, and they do not need to be the standard bearer for your company!

For example, companies like Rakuten Ichiba led by Hiroshi Mikitani, and Fast Retailing, owner of the now world-famous Uniqlo brand, led by Tadashi Yanai, have corporate cultures that are vastly different from the more traditional ones represented by, say, Mitsubishi Trading or NTT. Both Rakuten and Fast Retailing disrupted their respective industries with resounding success rather than supporting a traditional Japanese concept of "harmony." Their leaders value performance over seniority among staff, and stress English language acquisition as imperative for all, not just for those in the international department.

Some have said that Mikitani and Yanai are somehow uniquely "Western" in their thinking, but I disagree. It is only the degree to which both companies place value on things that are more typically emphasized in Western companies, like merit over seniority. However, this does not make the leaders "Western" in thinking any more than a leader of an American company, like Jeff Bezos of Amazon, who calls his company "customer-obsessed" is Japanese in his thinking, as Japanese concepts of customer service typically exceed those in any other country where I have lived. Jeff Bezos's business thinking may find resonance with concepts of customer service in Japan, but that is only coincidence. Jeff Bezos's thinking is simply his own thinking, and now Amazon thinking, and is neither Japanese nor American.

National culture or nationality has nothing to do with individual corporate culture. In fact, despite being oft-cited as a reason for why things cannot be changed in a Japanese company, I say emphatically here that there is no such thing as a "Japanese corporate culture." This is because there is no single corporate culture that describes every company in Japan. Companies like Rakuten and Fast Retailing are vastly different from and yet just as Japanese as for example the more traditional Mitsubishi Trading and NTT. Mitsubishi and NTT are staffed and led mostly by Japanese people, who come from the same Japanese stock as those at Fast Retaling and Rakuten. So what makes them so different?

Countries don't create corporate culture. Leaders create corporate culture, and corporate culture always trumps national culture when it comes to behavior and performance – at least within the confines of the organization or job. If Rakuten's Mikitani and Fast Retailing's Yanai can create corporate cultures that are so far removed from what is considered "traditionally Japanese," others can as well, including you for your company, irrespective of where around the world you are based.

If you are a leader in a Japanese company, whether you are Japanese or not, you have the power to shape the corporate culture just as other leaders of Japanese companies have done. You are not beholden to whatever anyone tells you is Japanese. However, if you buy into the Galapagos myth, Galapagos thinking will fill the void you make for it and become the reality for your company. Galapagos in Japan is a self-imposed exile.

Don't buy into the Galapagos myth. It becomes an excuse for not changing, even when change is possible, creating or perpetuating refraction layers.

National Culture Tempers Behavior but Company Culture Determines Behavior

Company culture is an expression I hear leaders use a lot but, if asked, they can rarely define what they mean without using all sorts of soft, squishy language. In my view, culture is a common set of approved behaviors. To understand the culture of any group of people, no matter how large or small, you merely need to look at which behaviors are typically praised or rewarded in that group, which are typically criticized, and which are typically treated with indifference. So for example, a company that rewards coming up with and trying new approaches, even when they fail, has a culture that is very different from a company that rewards only successful results and penalizes failure. By the way, which company do you think is likely to be more innovative?

A company's culture always trumps national culture. It frequently surprises people when I say this, because some leaders feel that they are constrained by Japanese culture in terms of what they can expect from their Japanese teams. I am not saying that Japanese culture has no impact on the way people in companies behave. Japanese culture only tempers company culture, in the way a master sword maker tempers steel—hardened yet at the same time made more elastic to flex rather than break under stress. In business, Japanese culture works both for and against your objectives.

For example, Starbucks coffee shops in Japan in my opinion have better customer service and have a more peaceful environment than elsewhere in the world. Staff will bring your drink to your table when they can, take your tray for you when you are done, and call out orders in a sing-song way as opposed to shouting them out. The shops are cleaner than the ones in the US, and shelves and cases are meticulously maintained. Starbucks Japan benefits from some parts of Japanese culture. Yet, it is not Japanese culture alone that makes Starbucks what it is in Japan. At its core, the company has a culture that is oriented toward customers and conducive to a positive retail environment. Japanese culture merely makes that stronger. If you don't believe me, try walking into the many Japan-grown Starbucks copy cats and compare them. Japanese culture alone cannot make a business a star performer like Starbucks Japan. Similarly, Japanese culture alone cannot break a business either.

When a business's culture challenges a country's cultural norms, it is the country's culture that will bend and flex under the pressure of the business culture, particularly when that business culture is reinforced by good leadership. It is only under weak leadership that business culture bends and flexes to conform to prevailing national culture norms.

The reality is that business leaders in Japan are constantly challenging the status quo, discarding assumptions, and breaking the rules. They inspire like behavior and attitudes among the people they lead. Some of the better known business leaders include people like Fast Retailing's Yanai and Rakuten's Mikitani, discussed above, but also people like Softbanks's Masayoshi Son, and Japan Airlines's reformist chairman, Kazuo Inamori. These are perhaps the most famous Japanese leaders today as I write this. Some non-Japanese leaders doing the same in the businesses they lead include Lenovo Japan's Rod Lappin, who oversaw one of Japan's most rapid and successful mergers of NEC's computer division with Lenovo. Godiva Japan's Jérôme Chouchan drives product innovation at Godiva Japan that is so compelling that products initially intended for the Japanese market are frequently adopted for markets worldwide. Renault-Nissan's Carlos Ghosn turned Nissan around and made it one of the most successful car companies in the world. Many leaders in Japan create norms of behavior in their companies that would be considered atypical among the Japanese, and you can do the same!

Business leaders who challenge the status quo in Japan are not a new phenomenon. Soichiro Honda chose to ignore ministerial "guidance" (*voir* orders) to stick to making motorcycles and not start making cars. Success was perhaps his best retort. Sony's founder Akio Morita set up Sony's first office in a bombed-out department store in Tokyo. Japanese industry was not built by business leaders who accepted the status quo. Japan was and still is built by mavericks and rebels, and the same is true of the real innovators and business success stories globally. The most successful business leaders reject or ignore the status quo. They do not simply surrender to cultural norms in pursuit of the average, and neither should you!

What Makes People Tick—Even the Japanese!

I am an amateur photographer. The thing that amazes me about photography is that a photograph of the same subject can appear so different depending on the camera, the lens, the lens filter, the type and sensitivity of the film or digital sensor, the settings of shutter speed and aperture, the preferences and skill of the photographer, and the agility of the camera to capture a subject. The camera itself renders only an interpretation of light and shadow, not reality itself. Any camera can take any photograph. It is just that the image a camera renders will be unique unto itself.

However, just because the image rendered may be unique, that does not make a camera unique. Every camera is fundamentally the same. In fact, the way a contemporary digital camera works is not that much different from a manual film camera. I can make my Leica M3 manual film camera, my digital Fujifilm camera, and even my iPhone produce wondrous photos for me with ease because, through experience, I have come to understand the fundamental ways of working that all cameras have in common.

People are a lot like cameras. We are so different from each other, yet we all work in fundamentally the same way. We see and interpret the same world so differently from each other. Like cameras, our lenses determine our frame, from a wide angle big picture to narrow close-up. What we see passes through filters that may block part of what we perceive. Just as film is sensitive to light that reaches it, so people have different sensitivities as to what they perceive and what they choose to take notice of in that perception; where some things may register and cause an individual to react, other things are less likely to do so or may not be noticed at all. We each have our capabilities to function. Based on what we see, some of us are able to act instantly to capture what we want, like a contemporary DSLR, whereas others require a slower, more considered approach, like a manual rangefinder camera.

Yet like cameras, all of which are designed to do one thing, capture an image, people also all function in fundamentally the same ways. We are all motivated by self-interest, whatever we may perceive that to be, even when we believe that it is in our best interest to contribute work in order to benefit the group. We all want to be prosperous, happy, healthy, and achieve a satisfying quality of life. We all want work that has meaning, that challenges us, and makes a contribution that others value. We all want to be rewarded for our work both monetarily and in expressions of gratitude or status. There is nothing that is fundamentally different or unique about any individual culture in this regard. In the same way my manual film cameras are not so different from my digital cameras, the Japanese are not so different from the Americans or any other people around the world.

The Problem is not the Local Culture—It's your Company's Culture!

In an initial meeting at the offices of one of my first Japanese client companies (and one of my best and longest-running business relationships), the CEO boomed, "My sales results from our new product are nearly nil. The sales people simply aren't performing. It's because they are Japanese! The problem is Japanese culture! There is no aggressive sales culture here!" Note that this CEO is Japanese himself!

"Well, your competitors appear to be selling aggressively and succeeding, and their sales force is just as Japanese as yours. What do you think is different?" I asked.

The problem was not that there is no aggressive sales culture in Japan as the CEO had asserted. Clearly, that is simply not the case. In fact, when it comes to a performance deficit, no matter what the type, culture is *never* the root cause. Let me repeat that, just so there is no mistake. National culture, whether that of Japan, the United States, France, or Australia, is *never* the root cause of a business problem. The root case is always in the *company's* culture. In this instance there was simply no sense of urgency in the *company's* sales culture. And a CEO is eminently capable of changing that! Countries don't make company culture. Leaders do.

So, how do you change a company's culture? Cultural change is always achieved through change in process, change in perception, and enlightenment. If you can help someone see a way of doing things that better serves them individually, they will change their behavior. Change the way people see the world, how they make sense of what they see, and give them an alternative model of acting that gets results, and you can change behavior, no matter what the nationality or the culture. Any pre-existing culture in any organization, whether Japanese or not, is merely a starting point for that change.

FIGURE 2.1 Behavior change cycle

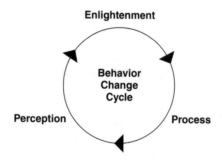

In other words, change in perception leads to enlightenment. Enlightenment causes people to change the process. Attempting new processes and seeing the results changes perception. Note that process, perception, and enlightenment influence each other in a circular manner—a virtuous or potentially a vicious circle. You can begin at any point in this circle to achieve the change desired. However, you must address all three in order to cement change.

So, take for example the time I was working with a Japanese sales team, in which there was a sales manager who insisted that it takes six weeks of meetings to determine if the potential customer contact in the company has independent decision-making power over a purchase. He explained to me that this process cannot be speeded up because, "This is the thorough way it is done in Japan!" as opposed to, say the United States, or elsewhere—not that this sales manager had ever worked outside of Japan! I did a role play with him, in Japanese, taking the part of the salesperson and having him realistically playing the customer prospect. I was able to make the determination using dialogue within three minutes—and that was only because I was taking my time! This was by no means a Japanese cultural problem. I demonstrated a process that gets results. Perception was immediately changed, and there was enlightenment.

The non-Japanese CEO of another company was struggling with his Japanese sales team over a product line that was a barely profitable commodity offering. He wanted to cut the line as it was a resource-hogging distraction from the company's core high-tech products that command high margins. The sales team insisted that in Japan, without selling the commodity products alongside the high-tech products, customers would stop buying the core product. The sales team simply refused to budge on this. I proposed raising prices on the commodity products to accurately reflect the company's costs, including its opportunity costs. The customers would naturally switch to another commodity supplier that was cheaper, but were still likely continue to purchase the unique product offerings as there were few options for alternatives, and the product provided excellent value. As a result of the pricing change, the commodity product line was wound down. No customers were lost except for those who had only purchased commodity products to begin with. The team continued to sell successfully, but as a result of the attrition in the commodities product line, they increasingly focused their attention on the more profitable high-tech products. Change in process led to change in perception, which led to enlightenment.

The Japanese CEO of a Japanese client company came to me for help with an innovation issue. He told me that the company had a product innovation team that had not come up with a breakthrough product in over ten years, and insisted that the reason was because they were Japanese: "They can't express individual ideas." I helped the team develop and document an ideation process with clear steps that they would execute periodically, but regularly. The first use resulted in 30 new product ideas, and the second in 60, when previously the team had been coming up with fewer than ten ideas per year! The company now has at least ten breakthrough development projects with real market potential that are beyond the ideation phase active at all times. A percentage of them will make it to market and will almost certainly succeed. This was a process problem, not a cultural problem.

As you read the examples above, you may be thinking, "That's pretty obvious. I could have thought of that and advised the same thing. And anyway, these kinds of problems come up in other countries too. They are not unique to Japan."

If you think so, you are exactly right. Any leader can achieve change by addressing process, perception, and enlightenment. There is nothing unique to Japan about any of these so-called "cultural" issues. If I had said the country was Germany, Malaysia, Australia, or even the United States, nothing that I described would have seemed particularly out of place. I challenge you to find a business problem that is uniquely "cultural" in nature. If you think you have one, you are not looking at it in terms of perception, process, and enlightenment, or focusing on how to change one of these as a start to reaching a solution.

In my experience, without exception, every change that is deemed impossible because "this is Japan," is possible. Even matters of government regulation! The American CEO of an online payment services was able to get the Japanese government to drop a regulation that was impeding his business, and a lot of others like his, despite their utility to Japanese society as a whole. Some people ascribed the regulation to Japanese close-mindedness and conservatism—a cultural problem if you will, if not simply one of pure prejudice. The CEO simply went to the Ministry of Economic

Trade and Industry, engaged with the decision makers there, explained the problem and, after a little bit of time, got the regulation changed. The law had been intended to block online gambling and paid pornography sites, not to bar a service valuable to society. A tiny bit of enlightenment in the right place, and the regulation was dropped in exchange for the formation of a self-regulating industry association with a clear set of standards, which the American CEO happily formed and led! Now, how easy do you think it would have been to get that kind of action in say the United States or France?

If the American CEO had bought into the idea that this was an immutable cultural problem, and not attempted to talk with Japanese government bureaucrats, the regulation would perhaps still be in effect now, the populace would have been deprived of a valuable service, and the CEO would have lost a critical business opportunity.

So-called cross-cultural problems are a red herring. They simply do not exist. Methods that lead to desired results are attractive to everyone. No matter what the context, achieving a change starts by reconfiguring the camera—address people's perception, enlighten, and give them a process to show them the way.

Sucking Air through Teeth: The Big Deal about Risk and Failure in Japan

Japanese people in general hate making mistakes of any kind, and are typically more sensitive to failure than people I have known in other countries. This tendency can manifest itself as being overly averse to business risk that others might view as reasonable and prudent, resistance to new ideas and new ways of doing things, and tentativeness in proposing ideas. This is not to say that people in other countries don't fear failure or making mistakes. However, in Japan the fear of failure is particularly acute.

For example, in the sales organization of a chemical company client, sales staff and managers alike resisted the idea proposed by the CEO to target new customers in different industries who use the kind of chemicals my client company produces, albeit for different purposes. Why? "Because we don't understand those industries and we have no reputation with companies in that industry, whereas we are experts in the industry of our current customers and are well-known. We might fail."

In another company, I was talking privately with a manager who discussed an idea he had for improving the business. It was a good idea, and I asked why he didn't propose it: "Well, what if it didn't work? I would be blamed for the failure."

This not to say that the Japanese have a worldwide monopoly on fear of failure. I have met American, Australian, French, British, and even Chinese people who have expressed similar misgivings. In Japan, however, the phenomenon is more acute. For example, the percentage of working people who start their own businesses in Japan is by far the lowest of all OECD countries. When I talk with would-be entrepreneurs and ask why they don't take the plunge, the answer is always, "What if I failed?"

However, what appears on the surface as aversion to failure is not actually that at all. Rather, the Japanese have a much greater sense of individual responsibility than you might encounter elsewhere. The expression to "take responsibility" in Japan carries a gravitas I rarely encounter elsewhere. At times, it can be extreme. Japan is the only country I know of that has a custom of ritualized suicide, *hara-kiri*.

This sense of individual responsibility in Japan manifests itself in positive ways too, not just negative ways. This is why you find Japanese public places clean, high levels of customer service in general everywhere, and lost wallets returned to their owners—with the money still inside!

If you want to change behavior, it is critical to appeal to the cause rather than the effect. So the way to overcome excessive risk aversion in Japan is not by attempting a rational discussion about the reality of the level of risk, the likelihood of bad things happening, and the real impact. This approach will fail because it is not the cause of the problem. If you want to reduce risk aversion, you do so by addressing individual responsibility, because therein lies the driver of the behavior.

For example, in working with a Japanese sales organization to help them reform their way of thinking about customers, processes, and sales objectives, at first the vice president of sales was outwardly skeptical—she viewed the ideas as "risky." She was more afraid of failure from trying something new than the inevitable failure resulting from doing things in the same way. Any debate about the soundness of the new approach fell on deaf ears. I addressed this not by attempting to reason about the soundness of the approach, but rather by framing her actions in terms of her individual responsibility. In this case, she was responsible for attempting new methods, not just achieving a successful result. Her managers confirmed that view of her responsibility. That worked. It was a change in her perception of her individual responsibility that resulted in enlightenment. Once enlightened, the process changed. Her execution was swift; she and her team followed through on their commitments, and even went above and beyond them! The business results came shortly after.

There is nothing about the Japanese that makes them inherently risk averse. Businesses and business people are constantly taking risks in Japan. Sony has bet the future of the company on optical technology. Fujifilm has bet the future of the company on digital cameras—with great success I might add. Toyota invested heavily in hybrid cars with a great result, and is now investing in fuel cell technology.

Even the members of the sales team resistant to approaching customers in different industries mentioned previously, are not inherently risk averse. In fact, some decades earlier, and still in the living memory of the senior managers, the company's sales people were constantly approaching new customers in unfamiliar industries and learning as they went. The R&D division was full of experts comfortable with going beyond their area of expertise and learning in order to support the sales people. The employees of the company had each felt individually responsible for moving outside their comfort zone. That had been the company's culture, and led to its success. Things only changed after the company found strong long-term success in one industry, in which it became increasingly entrenched. The only thing that had changed in the company over the years was the sense of responsibility of the managers and employees. Previously, people had been responsible for developing new markets for the company's products, for being adventurous, flexible, and for learning new things. More recently, people felt responsibility for supporting a specific industry, being an expert in its workings, and protecting the company's entrenched position within it. In other words, in the past, staff had been individually responsible for a type of behavior, not just successful results. What changed was that responsibility became confined to business results, and these results triumphed over specific desired behaviors. Once we were able to change the concept of responsibility to include behavior, change in the sales organization could take place, and it certainly did. The company developed relationships with customers in several new industries very soon after.

Where's the Bushido? Finding the Inner Warrior

People who say the Japanese are resistant to change ignore Japanese history. I know of no other country that has deliberately and successfully undergone as much change as Japan, and that change continues today. Prior to 1864, Japan was a pre-industrial feudal country that had closed itself to the outside world for two centuries, allowing foreign traders access to Japan only through a tiny island at the port of Nagasaki.

By 1904, a mere 40 years later, Japan was a power with which the major states had to reckon, having defeated the Russian Navy at Port Arthur, now Dalian, China. At the end of the Second World War, Japan was a country in ruin. Poverty and starvation were rampant, and industry was laid to waste. By 1964, a mere 19 years later, Japan was an industrial economic marvel on a par with other industrial powers on the world stage. Japanese people were healthy, prosperous, and peaceful. That year, Japan opened up the Tokaido Shinkansen line between Tokyo and Osaka—the world's only ultra-high-speed train at the time—and played host to the 1964 Olympics.

By the 1980s, Japan had gone from imitator to innovator, leading the world in manufacturing and other technologies. Prior to the 1980s, "Made in Japan" was synonymous with poor quality. Afterwards, it was a mark of excellence. Japan took over industries previously dominated by American companies, one after the other—automobiles, home electronics, semiconductors, among others. Japanese engineering excellence was so advanced that even American-designed Sidewinder air-to-air missiles, when manufactured by Japanese subcontractors, outperformed the same missiles manufactured in the US.

You cannot convince me that the Japanese are somehow inherently incapable of dramatic, rapid growth and change. The Japanese are in fact masters of change.

Don't believe the naysayers. Despite more than two decades of economic stagnation, Japan's standard of living has gone from great to even greater. Japan still has the lowest crime rate in the world of any advanced industrialized country, the highest rate of literacy, the lowest rate of poverty, a superb healthcare system to which all have access, and the longest life expectancy in the world. Other countries would consider themselves very lucky indeed to have Japan's "problems."

However, none of this seems to lift the spirits of the average Japanese person. Many long for the heady days of Japan's economic bubble and even Japan's golden age in the 1960s. When China's GDP surpassed Japan's in 2010, displacing Japan from number two in the world after the US, it only reinforced a feeling of a "has-been" country, now on the road to irrelevance. Hopelessness is on the rise, and many Japanese feel that there is simply something wrong with them as a people that cannot be helped. There is a general feeling of malaise felt everywhere as I write this.

This feeling can extend to mid-level managers in a company, as their businesses face a declining domestic market, increased competition from abroad, and a diminished stature in the world. "Sho ga nai," many Japanese will say, meaning "Nothing can be done about it." It is an expression of abdication, and also an excuse to take no action or attempt any change.

Wherever you are in the world, whether in a Great Britain still struggling with its diminished role in the world, in the US increasingly inward looking and socially fractured, or China, facing slowing growth and demographic change, don't buy into this kind of self-pity. Japan is the country that gave birth to *bushido*—the way of the warrior. It is a code of attitude and behavior of the *Samurai* class, but its ideals extend beyond the *Samurai*. Even today, hard work, self-sacrifice, fierce loyalty, working for the whole and greater good of the group, and never giving up persist. Scratch the surface a bit, and you will find this spirit still resides in most people. Whether it is the spirit of the settlers in the US, the great Victorian explorers in Britain, or the early explorers, inventors, and traders of China, all that is needed is a leader to bring it out, and that leader can be you. The rest of this book will show you how. You can also find additional resources at *www.relansa.co.jp*.

CHAPTER 3

Growth-Oriented Thinking – The Key to Anti-Refraction

S o, if managers whose thinking is dramatically different from that of the leaders above them creates refraction, what kind of thinking eliminates refraction or keeps refraction from forming in the first place? Growth-oriented thinking among managers is the key. This chapter discusses the characteristics and behavior of growth-oriented managers as they are the most adaptable and ready for change. These are as follows:

1. Action over perfection
2. Viewing failure as learning
3. Desire for personal growth
4. Comfort with ambiguity

These are all universal, and apply equally globally, including to Japan and the Japanese.

Action over Perfection

In working with several sales teams in a client company, with a brief to help them develop, many of the managers and staff talked of the need to "gather information" prior to taking any meaningful action. When different team members talked about new potential markets, customers, or applications for the company products, a frequent reason for not yet having taken action was "We don't have enough information." This reasoning was perfectly acceptable to the mid-level managers of the teams. When I asked specifically, "What information are you seeking? How will you use that information in determining the decision you make?", no one could answer me. A state of perpetual stasis reigned as a result of this constant, unfulfilled need for more data.

In a different engagement, I was working with a group of mid-level sales managers to help them develop methods for coaching sales staff. We did customer role play, a coaching technique that they would ultimately need to use with their own teams. In the customer role plays each manager spent a lot of time explaining products and making proposals, but asked very few questions about the customer's business. When I asked why this was so difficult, the answers were that they were not sure exactly what to ask and were afraid of looking foolish or angering the customer by asking something that they should have known. If the managers don't know how to ask questions of their prospects, how are the sales staff going to learn? If the managers see risk in asking questions, how do you think the sales staff will view asking questions?

At the same time, the sales managers complained that in sales meetings, they and their sales people had little idea of what customers wanted, and felt they never had enough market data to feel comfortable going into a meeting. This led to a stasis within the business; stasis that was continuously reinforced by a terrible vicious circle. Market data was never deemed sufficient to confidently pursue a direction in the conversation, leading to meandering monologues on the part of sales people hoping that something they say might hit home. Meetings with customers resulted in mediocre outcomes that also made sales managers and their sales staff feel deficient and question their own business acumen, making them even more hesitant to try new ideas or ask questions that would make them look stupid. This reluctance to ask questions even began to extend to internal meetings!

Chronic Information Insufficiency Syndrome is a term that I use for inaction due to a feeling of never knowing enough. It is a form of excessive risk aversion, and it is by no means confined to a sales function. For example, a senior executive coaching client was constantly having excellent ideas for new strategic moves—but he rarely put any of them into action. Why? "I just don't know enough to be assured that I would be successful. I need more information."

Yet, as in Japanese archery, you can be highly meticulous in setting up your shot, but you cannot be successful if you are striving for total perfection in your preparations. After all, eventually, you have to release and let your arrow fly, or otherwise you will never even attempt to hit your mark!

Many people have been educated to spew out the correct answers to predetermined questions. Learning answers by rote is not particular to Japan. It is common across Asia and can be seen around the world. However, only a very few of us have ever had much practice at formulating the right questions to ask in the first place. In Japan, the problems begin with the education system, where everything, including test problems, is well-structured. Questions are straightforward—How much? When? What? Where? What is the right way to ...? Few have been taught how to deal with unstructured problems, which require a different set of questions—Why? Why not? What if ...? What makes you say that?

Yet it is the latter set of questions that lead to effective action, to change, and to growth.

There is no such thing as a lack of information. If anything, we have too much information available to us, and many ways of getting even more. The real problem is not knowing what questions to ask, and having the courage to act on what you know at any given point in time. Google is utterly useless if you have no search terms available to you, or worse, if you have the wrong search terms that lead you completely astray. Meeting with an industry expert is a waste of time if you have no questions to pose. You can learn nothing from a new prospect if you spend all your time talking about your company and products without asking any questions about the prospect's business, goals, and pain points.

For example, in a role play with the group of managers I mentioned, one manager played the role of a real buyer in a customer company with which the relationship was shaky. The customer had decided to reduce their order for the next year. The desired outcome on the part of the sales person was to get a commitment for an increase. The buyer mentioned, "I noticed that you put our logo on the front page of your website as a place where consumers can purchase your products." The sales manager then went into a five-minute soliloquy on the company's website before I cut him off.

"Instead of simply talking, why don't you simply ask the buyer why he is bringing up the logo on the website?", I suggested. So he asked.

The person playing the role of buyer responded, "We get a lot of link traffic from your website, and we think that you have one of the best e-commerce sites in the industry. E-commerce is not our strength, and we were wondering if we could collaborate with you on e-commerce to help raise our sales."

There was a perceptible feeling of shock from the people in the room, with the realization that sales people were missing opportunities simply because they were not asking questions. Everyone was so busy trying not to appear ignorant, they missed out on simple pieces of highly valuable information on which to sell, which no amount of research or analysis prior to meeting with a customer could possibly have attained. When I asked the sales manager what keeps him from asking questions, he said "I don't want to be rude." Is there anything ruder than presuming that you do, could, or should know all that the customer values or is concerned about without asking directly?

In my days as a researcher, I had a Chinese colleague who talked about unstructured problems like this: "They're not valid problems. That's why I ignore them," he would state matter-of-factly. In academic research, you can get away with that. In business, however, structured problems appear only in MBA textbooks. Business in the real world is rarely if ever clean and neat, and that makes a lot of people feel uncomfortable. Many assume that it is they themselves who must be deficient in some way when unable to reduce a problem to such a set structure based on their own background knowledge and additional research from secondary sources. Because that is how most of us have been educated; the idea that a structured understanding will elude us is so difficult to conceive it can end up threatening our self-worth. However, nothing could be further from the truth. Most people can deal with the unstructured if they are willing to learn. It is merely their own tentativeness from lack of confidence that holds them back.

In addition, there is an implicit presumption that the correct way to obtain information is from researching published sources, whether reliable or not—internet searches, published information, market research reports, economic/demographic data, etc.—because this is primarily how people were taught to do research in school. The reality is that human intelligence always trumps secondary sources, is more targeted to specific needs, and rapidly acquired merely by asking questions. For example, in deciding whether or not a new product idea has legs before committing to investing in it, you can get rich and reliable information by meeting with or calling up ten or so current or prospect customers and asking a set of pointed questions, as opposed to purchasing market reports or performing aimless Google searches. Throw in a few people who may not be customers but who may have perspective on the market, like perhaps some key suppliers, and you will almost certainly have enough information to determine whether or not to progress to the next step—and this takes very little time! It is not necessary to rely on a marketing department to do this. Any manager can do this on their own, or it could easily become a team effort, raising morale and sending a signal as to the direction of future strategy and growth.

Viewing Failure as Learning

I have a friend who arrived in the US as a child around 1980. She was one of the many Vietnamese boat people who came to the US during that time. She is one of the most positive, optimistic people I know and extremely successful. She currently runs a successful business that she thought up and had the gumption to start. You also know or at least have heard of many people with similar stories. I have met such people in the US and in Australia—countries that both have a history of welcoming people from other countries.

In Australia, I knew a man who had made a multimillion dollar fortune in real estate development. He had migrated from China as a young man. He told me that when he first arrived, he lived in an apartment shared by many people like him. In his bedroom, there were bunk beds for six people. His path to success was neither smooth nor direct—he had gone bankrupt four times before his business succeeded.

What makes these people so successful has far less to do with intelligence, luck, possessions, or connections. Rather, it is that they don't fear failure. Many arrived in their new country with so little that they had nothing to lose by trying anything and everything to gain a foothold. Failure really meant little to them because the impact of the downside risk of failure was so low—it was not going to change their circumstances that much—whereas the upside gain was enormous. At the same time, the status quo for them was unsustainable. And, as a result, the impetus for improvement and change of *any* type is enormous.

I believe that people in such circumstances become conditioned to prefer rapid action over tentativeness. They gain a much more realistic perspective on the true impact of failure—that is to say that failure is rarely fatal and often beneficial. Failure for them is not a theoretical concept, as they have all failed many times at many of the things that they have attempted. However, if you talk with successful people about their failures, they all have one thing common—they value what they learned from the experience and could almost be said to covet more knowledge like it. They recognize that learning helped them grow and succeed, and without the failure, they may not have achieved as much.

In the end, it is the trait of viewing failure as part of learning and an inevitable part of ultimate success that is the marker of a growth-orientation and likelihood of success for people in general, and certainly it is the case with mid-level managers. Unfortunately, failure is often viewed as something to be avoided at all costs, something not to be discussed, and something to be ashamed of. This is the case in many countries around the world, but is particularly acute in Japan. The problem is, failure is a necessary part of growth and learning. Show me a manager who never fails, and I'll show you a manager who does not learn, does not grow, and merely occupies a spot on an org chart and is a tick in the headcount number. Show me a lot of managers who never fail and I will show you a business destined for stagnation and failure.

As I have discussed before, many mid-level managers have an exaggerated view of the impact of a potential failure. When a mid-level manager assesses risk, typically they will assess it from two perspectives—how it affects the company and the business and how it affects them personally. In my experience, exposure to personal risk always trumps what may be in the best interests of the company. So, for example, when I asked a mid-level sales manager in a Japanese firm why she was reluctant to develop new customer relationships, she explained that it was because they had no credit history with the company, and therefore might not pay an invoice. When I asked how often this scenario happens, she said she did not know of any specific case. When I asked whether sales managers are blamed for non-paying accounts, she did not think so, but thought that she might be blamed anyway. I asked if she were blamed, what the consequences might be. Would she be fired? She said it was possible. When I asked if that had ever happened to anyone else in the organization previously, she said no. Actually, this Japanese company rarely fired anyone, even for serious non-performance or worse. Yet, the sliver of a perceived personal risk was enough to keep her from taking action on new business. At the same time, there was little additional reward for her in seeking new business and not much in the way of consequences for not doing so.

When interviewing candidates for a mid-level or senior management position, I advise my clients to ask candidates to talk about a failure. People who view failure as learning are comfortable talking about their failures in brutally honest detail. As time passes, the story may even take on a comic aspect. However, critically, these people not only describe the failure, but always talk about what they learned from the experience and what they changed either about themselves or about how they do things. A candidate who responds in that way is much more likely to be learning- and growth-oriented. In Japan, people who are not learning- and growth-oriented, or perhaps less so, will either say they have never had a serious failure, or will talk about a trivial failure that is really a backhanded self-compliment to their ingenuity in resolving it—for example, saying that they nearly failed on a project for a customer because they worked too hard on it and came close to burning out, or something analogous to this. Such people don't view failure as learning, but as a permanent blight on their character. They will tend to be slow to learn to grow as managers, be tentative in decision making, avoid responsibility, and seek to blame others or unfair circumstances on their shortcomings—hardly the characteristics that you seek in a leader.

There is nothing wrong with failure. It is part of learning and growth. The only people that you need to avoid are those who fail without learning and who repeat the same mistakes over and over again. Your best managers are the ones who view failure as learning, don't fear failure, and covet the experiences gleaned from their failures, if not the failures themselves, because it is those failures that have made them successful.

Desire for Personal Growth

The CEO of a major snack food brand had to make a decision between two candidates for a marketing director position. One had significantly more experience than the other, but had spent over ten years in his previous job doing more or less the same thing, and wanted to continue that in his new job. The other had shown the ability to take on new responsibilities and acquire new capabilities rapidly, and had progressed through a series of jobs over the last ten years. The less experienced manager showed a consistent desire to learn, whereas the more experienced manager had become content with his current level of expertise, which was, indeed, significant.

The CEO asked me who he should hire. I advised hiring the less experienced manager. This was counter to the CEO's instinct, which was to hire the more experienced manager.

Whenever faced with a choice between an inexperienced learner who has desire for personal growth and a highly experienced expert who knows what is best and may be content with his capabilities, hire the learner. The reasoning is simple. Learners with a desire for personal growth constantly improve their personal capabilities. They tend to view change as an opportunity to grow and are willing to take risks to do so. They tend to become star performers. They also tend toward encouraging learning in their staff, and cultivate their reports' capabilities. They are not afraid of the promotion of other staff into their current position, because they themselves intend to grow and move on, and are confident in their own ability to do so.

People who have little desire for personal growth tend to calcify despite their talent and capabilities. They view any change as a threat as it may require development of new skills to maintain their own level of performance, and they tend to be resistant to change. They tend to avoid cultivating the capabilities of their staff, as they tend constantly to be on the lookout for upstarts from below gunning for their jobs. No matter how much of an expert they are to begin with, a manager who has little desire for personal growth will ultimately put a damper on organizational change and on growth of their staff. While they may seem like best fit at the time of hire because of the capabilities they bring to the organization, markets, customers, and business all change constantly, and when they inevitably do so, their capabilities will be mismatched. An organization is far better off with a group of inexperienced learners with a strong desire for personal growth, than a group of competent experts who feel they have nothing left to learn and little desire to grow.

Now, it is important to include a caveat here. There is absolutely nothing wrong with experience. Experienced specialists are necessary to any business in an economy that is knowledge driven. A business without specialists is not a viable one either. What I am pointing out, however, and this is perhaps where my message is a little more nuanced about failure, is that it all depends on the position that you seek to fill. And certainly anyone being considered for a management position should be someone familiar and comfortable with failure.

That CEO I mention above took my advice, and hired the inexperienced learner. He has been performing admirably, developing his capabilities as he goes. He is already bringing new ideas to the business, and cultivating the capabilities of his staff. He will, no doubt, become a star.

It is a good thing the CEO hired the learner, as the nature of the business is changing dramatically this year, and so are the required capabilities of the marketing director. Had the CEO had to make the hiring decision today, both candidates would have been on far more equal footing in terms of experience. Hire the learners. They enable organizations to change.

Comfort with Ambiguity

The higher the position of leadership, the greater the ambiguity. A capable manager must be comfortable with ambiguity in order to succeed. I define "comfort with ambiguity" as a calm confidence in one's own ability to succeed at an endeavor before knowing how to do so or what doing so might entail. It's a confidence in one's own ability to learn rapidly and overcome any obstacle.

For example, I had a client who was a sales manager overseeing about ten staff and who was promoted to vice president, overseeing a dozen sales managers and nearly 200 staff. She was tasked with completely restructuring the sales organization in a way that had never been done before. Changes in processes, sales people behaviors, and means of holding people accountable would be, without a doubt, necessary given the scope of the strategic vision presented to her; but she had no idea at the time what these changes might be in practice, much less how to achieve the change among the staff and managers of the entire sales division. That's what I mean by ambiguity.

Many people thought the task was impossible, but she was not discouraged. It would have been far less risky to her career to simply continue as a sales manager. After all, if she failed, a demotion back to her previous position within the company would have been the most positive outcome. Despite all the unknowns and the real risk involved she was undeterred. She did not know whether she could succeed, but believed that she could. And that was enough. She accepted the position. That's what I mean by comfort with ambiguity. The more senior the position, the greater the impact of the "what" and the ambiguity of the "how."

I serve as an adviser to Tsukuba International School in Japan. After the 3/11 Great Kanto earthquake and tsunami, the school lost nearly half its enrollment as expat families fled Japan. I helped the head of the school lead the school through the most difficult period in its history. As I looked through the strategic plans and budgets for the coming years, all I could see was conservativeness and defensiveness, presuming enrollment would continue to decline. However, for the school to thrive, enrollment needed to go up. At the time, it was not clear how the school would attain that enrollment. The school board members overwhelmingly insisted on a strategy. I insisted that the plans be revised to accommodate enrollment growth, even though growth at the time was viewed as highly unlikely, as increased enrollment was really the only option for success. The "how" could be sorted out later. Plans based on an assumption of continued decline were really only defensive, cost-cutting measures designed to prolong an agonizing march toward insolvency. Not knowing the "how" but still being able to plan for success, even as growth felt like a pipe-dream at the time, required a high level of comfort with ambiguity. The head of school eventually found that capacity within her, and led the school toward its vision. It was a good thing she did so, because within two years, enrollment more than doubled and was on the way toward tripling. The school had prepared options to purchase land, and gained financing for an additional building to house a gym and science labs. Had the school not been prepared for that contingency, it would have failed as a result of success. Discomfort with ambiguity results in preparation for failure, which can become a self-fulfilling prophecy. Comfort with ambiguity results in preparing for success. The mere preparation for success enables people to fill in the "how."

How Can You Tell?

Clients often ask me how to tell if a manager is growth-oriented or not. Many have had experience with promoting someone into a position and then regretting having done so, or making a poor choice in hiring. The damage caused by a manager who is not growth-oriented can be absolutely devastating to a business, the least of which is the amount of money you pay the person in terms of their remuneration and your time invested. Lost productivity and sales, lost opportunity for new customers and new growth, other departments or offices that struggle to collaborate with the manager's team and fail to reach their own targets and potential, the time of the manager's superiors consumed by issues emanating from the manager directly as well as from his team, lost time allowing competitors to move in, and so on, represent orders of magnitude of lost value beyond the mere cost of remunerating a non-performing manager. In addition, the phenomenon of refraction will have an impact on all staff below the manager. Growth-oriented staff and star performers under the manager cannot thrive and may lose all energy and enthusiasm, and possibly leave out of frustration. And this happens even in Japan, despite the reputation of the Japanese to remain loyal to one company their entire lives, good people quit their jobs to pursue more interesting opportunities, or otherwise simply not to suffer in a job without joy. Promoting the mediocre drives away the excellent.

You can distinguish growth-oriented managers from those who are not from their behavior. Below is a table comparing some typical behavioral differences between growth-oriented managers and managers who are not growth-oriented.

If a manager has been in your organization for any significant period of time, they should be a known quantity. I am often asked whether or not a manager who has not exhibited much in terms of growth-oriented

TABLE 3.1 Growth-oriented versus non growth-oriented manager behaviors

Non growth-oriented behaviors	Growth-oriented behaviors
Seeking permission or approval from above before acting	Reporting decisions made and actions taken
Warning superiors of every possible problem and pitfall as a way to cover oneself when failure occurs	Reporting planned approaches to problems and risks, and explaining the rationale of the approach chosen if asked, or otherwise making a recommendation for action
Waiting for orders from above	Independently moving forward toward goals
Avoiding any risk of failure even if it means inaction	Accepting failure as a possibility, owning up to it, learning from it, and moving on quickly without obsessive post-mortem or recrimination
Avoiding making decisions to avoid responsibility for failure	Recognizing that no decision is a decision in itself, and always the least optimal one
Perpetual information gathering	Willingness to act on best information at the time
Worrying about future should the wrong decision be made	Prepares for a future based on the assumption that the right decision will be made
Prepares only contingencies for failure	Prepares contingencies for success
Talks about one's job in terms of one's own internal responsibilities	Talks about job in terms of impact to customers, markets, sales, profit, and competitiveness, no matter what the internal role may be

behavior might change if put into a new position with greater prestige, responsibility, salary, or incentive pay. While I never rule out anyone's capacity to improve and change, I have rarely seen someone who is not oriented toward growth suddenly become growth-oriented when placed in a new position. Growth-orientation is not a skill. It's a personal value. A person is growth-oriented because it is part of their fundamental belief of how a person should live life. I have never witnessed anyone change their values or beliefs by virtue of a promotion or promise of incentive pay. All that happens is that they find new problems to identify and flag, new information to gather, etc. and the patterns of behavior established in their previous role are repeated in the new one.

Change in beliefs requires something much deeper—more often than not a crisis that shakes someone to their core. For example, I have a friend who is an extremely successful business person, and always has been, even though through a good part of his life he was succeeding in business while either drunk, high, or both. It was only when his lifestyle hit a crisis point that he changed. He is still as successful now, albeit as a far happier and fulfilled person. While this example may be extreme, when it comes to more ordinary mid-level managers, it is typically a crisis or a particularly revealing experience that causes them to change their values and beliefs. For example, unexpectedly losing a job for whatever reason with family to support and a mortgage to pay, and striking out as an entrepreneur. These kinds of experiences are transformative. Promotion and incentive pay are not. The biggest mistake I see leaders make is putting a manager who is not growth-oriented into a higher position of leadership, expecting them to rise to the task. Most of the time, this simply does not work. The less experienced manager who values personal growth and acts on that value continuously will always outperform managers who may be more experienced and even more skilled, but do not value personal growth.

The Resilient Manager

I once had the pleasure of meeting a man who was a CIA operative carrying out missions in the jungle (I won't mention where) during the Vietnam War. Twenty years on, he was an entrepreneur. On the subject of risk and fear, he told me, "Nothing is worse than being chased through the jungle being shot at. Business risk does not scare me." That's an unusually wide frame of reference and perspective, and while very few mid-level managers have ever been chased through a jungle as bullets whiz by their ears, they can treat simple challenges as if they might be in just such a situation.

Unless you live in a place like North Korea, the environment doesn't prevent people from growing. People prevent themselves. What makes a person hold themselves back can be traced to one common cause: fear. What are people so afraid of? Typically three things: rejection, looking stupid (or perhaps loss of status if you prefer), and failure. What makes the growth-oriented manager different is that they see these things as ephemeral, whereas the manager who is not growth-oriented sees them as permanent scars. Every setback is an invalidation of self-worth, and thus all challenges are avoided so as to preclude even the possibility. Better to have no incidents of failure. Yet lack of failure is no indicator of success. Indeed, you show me someone who has never failed and I'll show you someone who does not learn and grow.

The manager who is not growth-oriented is driven primarily by fear. That is not to say that growth-oriented people do not experience fear, even irrational fear—like fear of giving a talk as opposed to fear of being chased through the jungle by angry people with guns. Growth-oriented managers know how to co-exist with their fears, and not allow fear to drive their decisions, and that can result in deflecting or refracting waves of change from above.

Growth-oriented managers require no external validation of their self-worth to believe in their value to the world. They know their value and believe in it. They understand that neither success nor failure are permanent states, and that understanding frees them to do great things because a single failure does not daunt them, and they are unafraid to assume reasonable business risk or personal risk in their careers as managers. These are the people you need in mid-level positions in your organization in order to change the organization. They keep refraction from forming.

For additional resources on growth-oriented thinking, visit my website at *www.relansa.co.jp*.

CHAPTER 4

The Zen of Hiring

The last two chapters focused on eliminating refraction layers through changes to thinking, perspective, and mindset—the theme of the first part of this book. With Chapters 4, 5, 6, and 7, I move on to eliminating refraction through current business practices. Chapter 4 addresses hiring. Chapter 5 addresses eliminating overprotection of labor. Chapter 6 discusses goal-orientation over process-orientation. Chapter 7 is all about closing performance gaps. So let's get started.

In the previous chapter, I discussed the characteristics of growth-oriented managers who tend not to become part of refraction layers. "Where can I find such managers?", you may ask. In this chapter, I provide insights into where they exist and who they are. It is up to you to go get them!

Hire the Three W's: The Worldly, the Weird, and Women

Fulvio Guarneri, CEO of Unilever Japan, summed up his hiring strategy as the "The Three W's—western, weird, and women." Personally, I prefer to use the first "W" to stand for "worldly" as opposed to "Western," as the meaning behind "Western" is simply to hire people who speak foreign languages, particularly English, and who feel comfortable interacting with the world outside of Japan, or even better, enjoy doing so.

Fulvio Guarneri made this policy for two reasons. First, he wanted to diversify thinking by bringing in a more diverse group of people as opposed to the male graduates of top universities, seeking a lifetime salaried job with a top flight company, who were traditionally coveted by Japanese firms. Second, he wanted to tap into an underemployed and undervalued pool of workers.

Now, before I get a heap of emails pointing out how this policy sounds discriminatory, let me just clarify that this policy is not about excluding male graduates from top flight universities who do not have language skills or the tendency to look outside of Japan. That group has as fair a shot at being hired by Unilever as anyone else. What Fulvio Guarneri did was to level the field and by way of his direct dictum, expand the range of candidates to include qualified people with valuable capabilities who are often deliberately excluded by other companies in Japan.

The Three W's challenge the notion that somehow not seeking the traditional male graduate of a top tier university is a compromise of some type. On the contrary, it is a tremendous gain, and can serve to create and fuel a competitive advantage. I mean this not just for foreign companies in Japan. I advise leaders of Japanese companies to do the same. Leaders of small- to medium-sized businesses in Japan frequently complain to me that they never have first pick of the top graduates, and end up hiring people who they feel are less capable—that is to say, hiring male graduates from second-tier universities seeking lifetime employment in salaried jobs. Yet, this is a self-imposed disadvantage because of limits placed by these same leaders on who is an acceptable candidate. If women are not seriously considered for a career management track, if people who took time after college to travel the world or serve in a volunteer service organization like the peace corps are considered unreliable and out of step because they chose an unusual path and are two years older than other graduate new-hires, and if Japanese people who have been raised and educated overseas, fluent in other languages, are no longer considered capable of functioning within the framework of Japanese society, that's cutting out a large portion of available talent in Japan!

Rather than taking the Three W's as a prescription for whom to hire, treat the Three W's as a metaphor for seeking talent beyond restrictive traditional models. While each person is an individual, those who do not fit the norm tend to be the best agents of growth and change in an organization. A person who has made all the right moves in terms of education, and conforming to the expectations and norms of any given society is unlikely to be someone bucking for growth and change within an organization, much less being receptive to it. For those people who have bought into the traditional Japanese social contract—good school and conforming behavior in exchange for lifetime employment in a prestigious company and seniority-based promotion that will almost certainly be exacerbated as a result of the nature of the social contract in question—it is even more unlikely that they will exhibit the kind dynamism that you seek.

As a leader, it is up to you to establish the values of your organization, and attract people who are excited by those values because it is how they think as well. When you are building a company from scratch, you can do this yourself. However, most of the CEOs out there, and certainly almost all with whom I work, have inherited an organization in motion, whose ways of doing things has been established by their predecessors, or otherwise simply evolved based on what staff believed were the norms when guidance from above was absent. Don't let an HR manager dictate to you, the leader, the kind of people that are desirable and those who are not, no matter how well-intentioned. Be like Fulvio Guarneri. Decide what your Three W's are.

Whether you are leading an organization in Japan or somewhere else in the world, ask yourself what your Three W's are. What talent around you is easily dismissed or taken for granted?

The Worldly: English Ability Is Great, but It's the Mindset That Counts!

Many Japanese consider that being international, or worldly, is all about mastering English, and that mastering English is about memorizing a hodgepodge of vocabulary, and the correct grammar to assemble sentences. By virtue of this mastery, one is transformed into an international person, certified by some kind of English proficiency test like the TOEIC. I will not argue that learning English, or any language other than your own, does not improve international capabilities. On the contrary, I am personally a strong advocate of foreign language learning, even for people who already speak the world's lingua franca, English. However, mastering the mechanics of a language is only the beginning, and is perhaps not even the most important component in being an international citizen. For to truly be a global or worldly person means that you are able to work with people from other countries and cultures, even though you may not even speak a common language, or speak one with difficulty. That requires openness to other people in the world. It requires keen skills of observation, a perceptiveness of what drives people's behavior beyond the norms to which you are accustomed in your own culture. It requires suspending your assumptions, and having a curiosity about the world around you. You need not only have insight on the differences between people, but also about what makes us all the same, for it is on what binds us together that relationships are constructed. Learning a foreign language is a means to that end, because in the process of attempting to master a language, chances are that you will exercise your capabilities for spotting commonalities among the myriad of differences, and begin to look at the world in a different way. Truly international people see beyond the differences that they perceive, whether cultural or behavioral, because they realize that these differences are largely superficial. Rather, it is the commonality of values that all people share that is important, no matter where we are from, and it is upon these common-alities that we build international relationships.

However, learning a language is not the only way to develop one's own international capabilities, and just because you learn a language does not necessarily mean that you are worldly. I have met many Japa-nese who speak English functionally well, yet who remain provincial, even xenophobic in their thinking. For example, a mid-level manager in a client company of mine speaks English better that most managers in Japan whom I encounter. Yet at the same time, in every workshop and meeting in which he participated, he could not help himself explaining in excruciating detail why something would not work "because we are Japanese," or how an idea that I proposed "would never work in Japan," because it represents "Western thinking." At other times he would say, "You know, the reason we have this problem in Japan is because we are Japanese. This is the way Japanese are, so what you suggest as a solution might work in America, but not here."

"What makes you think that American businesses don't have the same problem?" I would ask earnestly. And this is the crux of it—be wary of anyone around the world who claims that a business is unique because it is, for example, Chinese, or that a solution will not work because you are working in the context of a Polish company that has won an outsourcing program. What appears to be an issue of cultural norms tied to a country is more often than not you coming up against the culture of the organization itself. And it is always possible to change the culture of an organization.

In working with a CEO with a foreign bank in Japan, who was grooming a Japanese executive manager to be his successor, he confided in me that his biggest concern was that his successor "doesn't believe that non-Japanese can successfully work with a Japanese team in a C-level position." The executive manager speaks fluent English, but his thinking could hardly be considered worldly. A manager who speaks fluent Eng-lish is of no use to your business if at the same time they are xenophobic, harbor prejudices against non-Japanese, and prefer to do deals with the world outside Japan at a distance, and then only when they absolutely must. Truly worldly people exhibit curiosity about the world beyond the country in which they live, and they satisfy it not only through travel and language learning, but also through consumption of cultural products, such as books, films, enjoyment of artwork, events, and food.

The mindset that must accompany English ability is one of curiosity about and openness toward the world and its people. When I say "English" mindset, I am speaking about a kind of worldly outlook. However, just as mastery of English in a technical sense does not guarantee a worldly outlook for a Japanese person, the same is true of anyone else in the world, including native speakers of English! It is possible to be a native speaker of English and be xenophobic, lack curiosity about other people and places in the world, and have a sense that "foreigners" are somehow too different to deal with comfortably. It is also possible to have a worldly outlook and attitude as a Japanese speaker as well. Indeed, this mindset is a prerequisite for the ability to work with others, even when there is no common language, or one with which one or both parties may struggle.

English ability is fundamentally a technical skill—a tool that is a means to another end; and while essential to growing international businesses, including most businesses in Japan, an English skill means little without an accompanying worldly mindset. Seek people who have a worldly mindset, and not just an English skill. Better yet, give priority to the mindset, because people with the right mindset can learn English, whereas those without the mindset will always work to hold the outside world at bay, no matter what their English ability.

The Weird: Tall Poppies and Protruding Nails

There is a Japanese proverb that you will almost certainly never have heard—"The nail that sticks up gets hammered down." This is a cautionary proverb, and sometimes an admonishment, advising people to conform and not stick out or stray from what is considered "normal." More than most, I have found that the Japanese value sameness. On school classroom walls, you will often find "We advance together as a class." In Japan, to be called "ordinary" (*futsu*) is not pejorative. In fact, if you are told in Japanese that "you are not ordinary," this is not to be taken as a compliment.

This is not to say that the Japanese have a monopoly on conformity or normative behavior. In Australia and New Zealand, there is a similar expression—"Tall poppies get their heads cut off." Whereas in Japan, the nail that sticks up is about being different, in Australia and New Zealand, tall poppies are about people who exhibit excellence a cut about the rest. No matter what the nuances are, both are expressions of values that tend to create a gravitational pull toward mediocrity.

One of my clients in Japan is Mikado Kyowa Seed, part of the Limagrain Group out of France, the fourth largest supplier of agricultural seed in the world. The company is staffed by many mid-level managers who in their youth, rather than seeking a typical salaryman job fresh out of university, volunteered with the Japan International Cooperation Agency or JAICA, a non-government organization that provides support for developing countries, much like the Peace Corps in the US. As JAICA volunteers, they went to developing countries in Africa, South America, and Asia and helped people improve agricultural practices and increase crop yields for a few years before returning to Japan. A lot of Japanese companies would not even consider hiring these people. They are already out of step with their peers, and likely think differently from them. Their boldness in pursuing their own path bodes ill for the organization seeking salaryman automatons whose personal ambitions and desire to contribute to and perhaps improve the world around them take a back seat. If you want people who think differently and aren't afraid to be different, it's best to hire people who have behaved that way in the past.

I once worked with the division head of a major Japanese IT company—a very smart guy. He had innovative ideas about IT and was not afraid to break convention to try something new, or even pay for staff to do research and development—even though the division's primary purpose was service delivery and, as a manager, he had profit/loss responsibility. I liked him a lot. He spoke very good English, and was highly articulate. I was surprised when he told me he taught himself English— he had not studied abroad or spent significant time overseas. I found this a remarkable feat, and believe this manager to be extraordinary. His staff, who are fond of him as a boss, told me outright that they thought he was "weird," and not weird in a nice way. They nicknamed him *hentai,* which literally means "pervert," and can refer to anyone who is considered to be an aberration—all in good fun, of course. Still, I have found that when people are derisive about someone in a good-humored way, there is always a streak of ill-humored truth revealed. People were somewhat suspicious of him for being so different in that he had mastered English on his own, where most others had failed or not even tried. This manager, however "weird" he may have been, was nonetheless achieving extraordinary results for this company, and pushing the envelope of the organization's capabilities. If this is perversion, many companies would be lucky to count such "perverts" among their numbers.

I met a senior vice president of a Japanese medium-sized business. He was always curious, and looking to learn more about anything that he thought could help the business. He would ask my advice on strategy, leadership, and organizational behavior. His English was only just ok, but from time to time he would use English with me simply because he likes English and wanted to improve his ability. A Japanese male, middle-aged, mid-level manager who told his peers that he "likes" English might get the same reactions as someone who says he likes tax-accounting, albeit in a room full of non-accountants and not being an accountant himself. As I got to know him better he told me how, in his youth, he had gone to school with, and was friends with, a son of the founder of the business. After school, the two friends took off to South America together and started an export trading business in alpaca wool products. Now that's pretty weird for anyone, not just for someone who ends up as a salary-man, and a senior-level one at that. The connection with the son of the business's founder led him to the job after the two had returned to Japan. The son of course would have always had a position waiting for him in the business if he wanted it, but for his friend it would have been difficult to find a good white-collar job after his experience in South America. The company was lucky to have hired him. He is one of the top performers in the business, has generated immeasurable value for the business, and serves on the company's board of directors. The only irony is that it is unlikely that the same company would have hired him if it were not for the connection with the founder's son. He would not have even made the HR director's first cut because he is so unusual. Fortunately, it is not HR that makes all decisions in the company. Managers in the company have great influence over who to hire, even among the graduate candidates. In fact, the company organizes social gatherings between candidates and managers specifically for managers to get to know the candidates better. While this seems like common sense, it is unusual in Japan. It makes you wonder how many businesses have lost opportunities to generate much value, simply because some of the most capable people are considered too weird for employment.

By what criteria is your HR department making first cuts of candidates? How much sway do your line managers have over new-hires?

What kind of people are there out there who might be considered weird by others, but dynamic by you? How much additional value could your business be generating by hiring weird people that other employers dismiss out-of-hand? What is your HR department doing in evaluating candidates? What are your managers doing? Who is your organization cutting who might otherwise serve as a force for growth and change, when and where needed in your business?

Salarywoman

Women are woefully underemployed in Japan. In fact, Japan could resolve much of its low-growth problems simply by increasing employment of women. Traditional Japanese companies tend to prefer a male for management track positions whereas a woman has typically served in a uniformed clerical position, known as "office lady," or OL for short. Men have typically been offered lifetime employment, whereas women were expected to quit after marrying. Employees are often divided into two classes—*sogoshoku* and *ippanshoku,* both of which can be translated as "general work" using synonyms for "general." However, the former is meant for men in lifetime employment tracks, whereas the latter is meant for women in non-career positions. A Japanese manager in a more traditional Japanese firm once confided in me that the firm actively seeks to hire the prettiest *ippanshoku* women candidates: "It attracts the top male graduates, because a lot of young men find their wives among the OLs." For women who are looking for a husband who works for a prestigious company, and yes such women continue to exist, the system works for them. Those women who may be looking for more out of a job are simply out of luck.

In the past, career-oriented Japanese women either targeted foreign firms that had no explicit gender barriers, or otherwise left Japan to work abroad. Japanese women, more than Japanese men, tend to seek tertiary education overseas on their own initiative, whereas men are typically sent by their employers. A Japanese woman who seeks education overseas and returns to Japan with a worldly perspective and fluent English finds a natural home in foreign firms in Japan. Also, women who have had the courage to go overseas and the ambition to turn their learning into a career tend to be self-starters, and more dynamic than their male counterparts who went to a Japanese university and sought a salaryman position. These women are generally less afraid to explore and try new things. They are comfortable in an international environment. They have a curiosity about the world that is more acute than average, and they tend to enjoy learning. They are great candidates for a growth-oriented firm, Japanese or not.

For traditional companies though, such women can be a bit scary. They tend to think for themselves and speak their minds, and are less apt to conform. Such assertiveness is unusual in Japan in general, and assertiveness of any type is usually reserved for men, not women. A woman who is more assertive than her male counterparts can be off-putting at best and daunting at worst. Some men allow themselves to be intimidated by them, although there is really no rational reason for this. International business people tend to value assertiveness in general, and an assertive woman in a professional context tends to be less confronting to them, if confronting at all.

Ambitious women often prefer the opportunity offered by international firms as opposed to the confines of traditional domestic firms.

A lot has changed in Japan in the last 20 years. Both the lifetime employment system and gender barriers have begun to crumble and the system I describe above is in decline. Yet, vestiges remain today and Japan still has a long way to go.

The real opportunity is not just for those women with a penchant for English and education abroad, who are really a special case. It is also for the women who don't fit that mold, who are well educated at Japanese universities and have career ambitions, though not necessarily international ones. They tend to be overlooked by both international and traditional Japanese firms. Yet, these women are like gold for the firms that have the courage to hire them.

One of my Japanese client companies deliberately recruits women for career tracks—and not just those who speak fluent English and have studied abroad. The company tends to find a higher quality pool of candidates among women compared to men. In fact, a number of their top-performing sales managers and sales people are women. In working with the company over the years, I have found the women staff at all levels more open to change, more open to learning, and more open to improving their English. The company has a generous program in which they will send employees overseas for up to six months to study English at company expense while on salary, for employees who wish to do so.

It surprises me that anyone should not want to take the company up on this offer. Yet women employees take up this offer in numbers disproportionate to their male colleagues. The international division of the company has more women at higher levels than any other division in the company. On average, in that company, senior leaders have commented that the women employees perform better than the men. It's a wonder that more companies don't tap into this gold mine. What could possibly be holding them back?

For one thing, it is the attitude toward work–family balance. Traditionally, the salarymen work long hours, staying in the office until late at night. Going home at 9 or 10 p.m. is not unusual—although all this overtime is mostly for show. There is little productivity for the time put in. On top of that, there are *settai* and *tsukiai*—both of which are evening drinking sessions, the former being with customers and the latter with colleagues. These libation rituals are considered and essential part of work-life and business in Japan. The informal drinking sessions are used to develop rapport outside of rigid office settings, and inebriation, whether real or feigned, provides a cover for direct communication, which at times can be frank or blunt, and would be considered offensive in the context of communication between colleagues, but which is forgiven as a result of the context. These customs, while great for building rapport with customers and colleagues, are not conducive to building rapport with one's own family. In extreme cases, salarymen who spend a career in this way end up finding their wives and children alien to them, and have no idea what to do when they retire, having developed no real outside interests or passions. They mope about the house to the point where their wives refer to them as *sodaigomi*—literally oversized garbage, like an old washing machine, that annoyingly takes up space and gets in the way in a cramped Tokyo apartment until you can pay someone to haul it away to a dump.

The client company, mentioned above, that proactively recruits women for career tracks, and has reaped the rewards, has also changed what it means to be salaried, whether a man or a woman, in the company. There is little *settai* or *tsukiai*. Overtime is not encouraged. In fact, scheduling anything later than 6 p.m. is frowned upon. I once asked a company executive about this. His reply was, "A lot of our employees have kids to look after in the evening. Not having to work late is important to them, particularly to a lot of women who work here. We might lose our best staff if we required or encouraged people to work late, or go out late drinking."

In fact, none of the top executives I met drink at all—at least not when going out with employees, customers, or me. The only reason they don't, they say, is that they don't like to drink. They don't discourage others from drinking, but they demonstrate that they can conduct their business without drinking themselves, or the excesses of after-five outings in Japan. It sets the tone for the rest of the company. This does not mean that the people who work in this company never go out and never drink as part of their jobs, but they do it with a kind of judicious moderation that I don't often see in Japan.

I don't know any Japanese women who actually want to become "salarymen." After all, who wants all the extra baggage that entails? Yet, that doesn't mean that women don't want the same opportunities and respect afforded to their male colleagues and counterparts. Rather, what I find in Japan is that both men and women want a more balanced and fulfilling life. Both men and women want to pursue ambitions other than just professional ones, and grow in personal ways, not just professional ways. Men and women in Japan have to recognize that the old model of the salaryman simply does not fit in today, and is out of sync with society. Part of what has driven Japan in this direction is the increase in inclusion of women on career tracks in the workplace in Japanese companies, not just the foreign ones. It is ironically the rise of the *salarywoman* that is improving the lot of the salaryman.

If you want to make your workplace more attractive to women, start by making it more attractive to men. By that I mean offer paternity leave, not just maternity leave. Limit the overtime. Stop treating late-night drinking as the only meaningful way to conduct business and establish rapport with clients and staff. Make a decision not to drink during outings OK as opposed to antisocial or weird. Do those things as a start, and then reach out to women. Talented women and men will come in droves.

Gaijin and Other Red-Bearded Devils—Like Me!

I once attended a talk by the head of the Bank of Japan who was speaking on ways of sparking economic growth in Japan. Japan has a declining population. Each year there remain fewer people in the labor market, which has a negative impact on growth. One way of changing that is to make it easier for foreign nationals to migrate to Japan to work, much in the way Australia does. The head of the bank admitted that doing so would be undesirable for most Japanese, as it would alter the fabric of Japanese society. Japan has a funny relationship with all people and things that are foreign. On the one hand, the Japanese covet an American lifestyle, French fashion, Chinese food, and so on, but with a safe buffer in between these "desirables" and themselves.

On the other hand, many Japanese prefer to keep what is foreign at a distance and separate. I once walked into a local French Patisserie in Japan. The pastries in the window looked good. The name of the shop was Mont Saint Michel. I asked the Japanese patissier, why Mont Saint Michel? Had he ever been to it? He replied no, he had never been to France. I asked if he ever thought of going simply to learn new techniques and try the pastries there. He told me emphatically, "French pastries don't taste good. The Japanese ones are much better." I'm not sure how he knew, never having been to France. In any case, he had no interest in going to France, and believed nothing was to be learned there. While his pastries looked good, I found them bland and indistinct in taste.

Hiring non-Japanese to work in your firm is yet another way to capture great talent, while encouraging growth and change. After all, non-Japanese bring different ways of thinking and working. They challenge assumptions, and can serve as agents of change. They help an organization become more international simply by being present and working with people. They also potentially bring valuable skill sets from their professional experience and education overseas. Some skill sets are lacking in Japan, such as software engineering. Widening a pool of candidates to non-Japanese gives companies access to greater degrees of talent, and more of it.

When it comes to dealing with foreign people, however, I have found many Japanese struggle with this. They often make the "foreignness" of a non-Japanese counterpart the primary aspect of the person. They worry about problems in communication, food, and culture. Sometimes, they worry that foreign people will look down upon them for supposed inadequacies in Japan and the Japanese. This kind of thinking creates an implicit barrier between Japanese and non-Japanese, which in reality does not exist, nor has any reason to exist.

I have often found people in companies in Japan reluctant to hire foreigners for this reason. Ironically, some of these companies are the Japanese operations of foreign companies themselves! They are staffed by Japanese, who while working for a company that may find its head-quarters in Europe or the US, prefer no actual foreign colleagues in their midst! I once worked for an American company in Japan whose new Japanese CEO refused to have any non-Japanese in a customer-facing position. This was not a matter of language ability—it was simple exclusion based not on ability but on nationality. Indian software engineers were tolerated, but non-Japanese sales staff quickly found themselves out of a job. The company's sales results flagged during that CEO's tenure, and he later found himself looking for new work.

Other companies that do hire foreign staff may do so as a form of token internationalism—just to have a foreigner on staff. They don't expect so much in terms of contribution to the business, but rather the Japanese staff being influenced by having a foreigner around. Unfortunately, this has the wrong kind of influence as it reinforces an idea that a non-Japanese cannot contribute in a meaningful way in Japanese business. Some Japanese managers have trouble considering the abilities of a non-Japanese beyond being able to serve as a translator of English documents. These types of attitudes and practices work against a firm's ability to realize its full potential and achieve growth and change. Like avoiding the Three W's, excluding foreigners narrows options and forces suboptimal compromises in hiring choices.

If you want to grow your business and your business's organizational capability, consider hiring the outsider. For example, there are many non-Japanese graduating from Japanese universities with bachelor and master degrees who would love to have a successful career in Japan. They have drive. To study abroad, to obtain a foreign degree, is an indicator of drive, ability, and determination. Imagine what a team of such people in your business could do!

Loyalty Is Overrated; It's Disloyal People You Want!

Patriotism is the last refuge of the scoundrel—or so it has been said. Similarly, company loyalty is the last refuge of the mediocre. Are you really sure you want fervently loyal employees?

Disloyalty is not to be confused with treachery. They are not the same thing. Treachery means deliberately harming the organization to which you claim allegiance. Disloyalty means not allowing allegiance to an organization to be the sole driver of your personal decisions. A disloyal person will leave if they think it is in their own best interests, without malice or intent of deliberate harm. In a free market society, freedom of labor is natural. Leaving a firm for whatever reason is a right and within the rules of the game.

Your best employees are rarely the most loyal. They are the ones who are confident they can always get good work elsewhere whenever they want, and have no qualms doing so. They stay with your company because they *want* to stay, as opposed to those who feel they *must* stay, and are among the most committed. Employees who are sticking with your company because they are afraid to leave, even though they dislike their jobs, will be with you until the end of time, performing the very minimum necessary and never becoming your stars.

The irony is that the most committed of your employees are among the most disloyal. It's those who swear allegiance that you need to worry about. Mediocre employees tend to collect in a company like stagnant rainwater, whereas the best employees flow freely. Too often, I have heard managers tell me about how they used to have some great staff members, but they left for better opportunities, and they complain about the quality of the current staff that have remained. Yet, these same managers who then seek to hire new staff are suspicious of otherwise excellent candidates who have changed jobs, because they worry about their "loyalty." It does not seem to dawn on them that the excellent employee who left, who was great for their business, is also a job-changer in the eyes of another company. They believe that the new company who hired away their best is lucky for having done so, without recognizing that the job-changer sitting in front of them may be just as excellent, having left their former employer in search of a better opportunity.

The way to retain the best employees is to continuously invest in their development and provide them with opportunity. No excellent employee will ever shackle themselves to a firm that is not working for them out of some selfless rationale about loyalty.

So make no pretense about loyalty. Hire the disloyal, and do what it takes to retain them.

You can find additional resources on the topics discussed in this chapter and more at *www.relansa.co.jp*.

CHAPTER 5

Breaking the Iron Rice Bowl

L ifetime employment and seniority-based promotion, bedrocks of the traditional system of employment in Japan, are also one of the greatest causes of refraction layers of mid-level managers in companies. Any kind of overprotection of labor results in calcification. Among mid-level managers, calcification manifests itself as inflexibility toward change and brittleness—exert pressure to change on a calcified layer of managers, and they crack apart and crumble. Overprotection of labor in Japan as anywhere else in the world hampers the performance of any business.

Guarantee of lifetime employment (*shushin koyo sei*) in a single company is hard to imagine for many people outside of Japan. What is even harder to imagine is wanting to be in the same company for life. I am not disparaging people who have had long, fruitful careers in a company by choice, and I know a number of such people who had been employed by Hewlett Packard, IBM, and many others. For most people outside of Japan, changing companies several times in one lifetime is the norm. In fact, many people change careers and industries several times during their working lives. I doubt many outside of Japan would relish the idea of being with one employer forever—people change and so do companies. Many people have experienced a time when working with an employer is no longer fulfilling, and are no longer happy doing so. This is neither their fault nor the employer's. People evolve and move on.

When it comes to employment, the old social contract in Japan was based on guarantees of security. Go to the right elementary schools, and get into the right middle school. Go to the right middle school, and get into the right high school, and then the right university. Go the right university and get the right job in government, for the very elite, or in the private sector. The right job usually meant a lifetime employment job at a prestigious, household-name Japanese company—foreign companies don't count in this system.

In Japan, lifetime employment tends to go hand in hand with a system of seniority-based promotion (*nenko joretsu sei*). Advancement in both position and salary is for the most part guaranteed with only minor variation. However, more importantly, advancement based on merit that is out of step with seniority is against the rules. I have frequently been told by business leaders that they cannot possibly promote a star performer at this time because they would become the boss of people older than they are, or who have been with the company longer.

The merit of this system of dual guarantees, lifetime employment and seniority-based promotion, is that it was a way of attracting the most talented people to the company, primarily university graduates, as companies traditionally rarely hired anyone mid-career, assuming that is what the most talented people valued—guarantees. Like everything in life, upside potential for reward is always the currency for which reduction in risk is bargained. So, these elite graduates were, and still are to some degree, buying a guarantee for the good life, at the price of a possible extraordinary life. I don't blame the Japanese for this. This system developed during postwar Japan, at a time when conditions were very different from today. Just securing adequate housing was a challenge during the years after the Second World War, to say nothing of a steady income to feed one's family. To combat this, companies often offered housing as part of the job—a system that continues to this day but to less of a degree. Company housing with large companies in Japan is not uncommon.

The pressure from family to buy into this system can be enormous. An elderly Japanese friend of mine, who ultimately made a fortune in real estate as an entrepreneur had, as a young man, secured a job with Mitsubishi Trading, a prestigious company in Japan. He hated the job. The style of management echoed Japanese militarism according to him. He is a tall man and handsome with distinct features. As a young man, I suspect he was Adonis-like. One day, while swimming in the pool at the Imperial Hotel, he was called over to the pool side table by a man sitting with several people. The man told him he was a film director, and said my friend had the perfect build and features for a character in his next movie. He wanted to cast him. My friend, who was interested in acting, wanted to take up the offer, but his family refused to allow it. How could he possibly throw away his career at Mitsubishi for something as frivolous as movie making? Having a son at Mitsubishi gave his family social standing in addition to the guaranteed income. The movie director visited my friend's boss at Mitsubishi Trading in an attempt to persuade him to "release" my friend from his employment. The director visited three times to no avail. In the end, he gave up, and so went my friend's dreams of acting. Who knows what could have been? The movie director was none other than the world-famous Seiji Kurosawa.

Japan is in the throes of change. In today's Japan, lifetime employment and seniority-based promotion could be viewed as being simply unethical.

Nearly two decades of recession in Japan, while chipping away at the system, have resulted in a generation of underemployed and unemployable people. As graduates found themselves without regular salaried jobs waiting for them, they had to compromise, taking part-time jobs or no jobs at all. Companies had guaranteed employment to the previous generations and simply did not have the need for new talent, even though a lot of the current talent was not really providing value to the company. After a few years, many of this recession generation found themselves out of step with people their own age who had secured employment. Even though companies now need fresh talent, many of these people found they had simply missed the boat—they are now too inexperienced to be considered for mid-career employment and too old to be considered as graduate hires. They are in a catch-22 predicament, and have been given the moniker of "the lost generation."

Some Japanese companies resorted to highly unethical behavior. One top-name Japanese company had to transfer non-productive mid-level managers from white-collar positions in the head office in Tokyo to manual labor positions at warehouses in the outskirts of Tokyo, loading heavy boxes product onto delivery trucks. Many lacked the physical condition for the work. Most were in their fifties. Rather than laying off these employees in some reasonably humane way, the company's strategy seemed to be to make life so unbearable for them so as to make them resign of their own accord. Some ended up with serious physical injuries. Yet, the lifetime employment guarantee was upheld—at least nominally.

The result was the end of the implicit social contract in Japan—work hard, excel at school, and get a lifetime guarantee if you are among the best. Social changes have resulted in a shift in attitude among the younger generation. We have seen a rise in what are known as "freeters"— young people who have no particular career ambition at all. They move from one low-skill part-time job to the next, live with their parents or in low-rent apartments, avoid consumption, and can't even consider marrying and raising a family, exacerbating Japan's declining population problem. We have also seen the rise of what are called "herbivore men"—men with no career drive. They simply graze on the field of low-skill jobs, showing little interest in dating women—a stark contrast to the image of the unstoppable carnivorous salarymen of the 1980s.

Many companies in Japan have abandoned lifetime employment and seniority-based promotion—at least nominally. However, in practice the system continues in the form of reluctance to fire people even when justified, the hiring mostly of new graduates and spurning of mid-career hires, and squeamishness at promoting someone beyond their seniority. The system continues, and may even be present in your business under the surface. Surprisingly, I have found that even in foreign firms in Japan, while there may be no explicit policy in favor of lifetime employment and seniority-based promotion, the practice exists.

The results for your business can be grave. After all, why expend effort on top performance if it goes unrecognized? There is little reward for success. You may even suffer retribution for attempting to outshine your boss and your peers. At the same time, penalty for failure still exists. Better to keep one's head down, do the minimum to maintain a minimum acceptable level of performance, and do little to risk any kind of possible failure.

For people who are driven because ambition is in their nature, they may simply choose to leave your company, to go somewhere where their talents are respected, appreciated, and rewarded—and yes, these companies do exist in Japan. Talented people have options and are unafraid to exercise them. If your company tends toward protecting the mediocre, the excellent will flee.

The system also creates refraction layers—like layers of sedimentary rock, each entering generation of new-hires calcifies. They create layers of group thinking, conservatism, and resistance to change, as they are always rewarded simply for passing time in the company, not for necessarily achieving anything of business value. They become a barrier to change from below, and from above.

Heisei Restoration

It is a new day in Japan—*Heisei*, the name of this period under the current emperor, means peace and prosperity, and Japan has achieved both. It is not necessary to be shackled to a system whose design was based on the exigencies of poverty and the concerns of a people reeling from decades of political instability and war. As business leader, do not allow any of your advisers to dictate to you that lifetime employment and seniority-based promotion are required for success in Japan.

The friend I mentioned earlier—the could-have-been Kurosawa movie star—as a teenager just after the war, made money for his family by transporting fish from a rural fishing village to Tokyo and selling it to people with hungry families. Through lucky circumstances, he got himself a job as a busboy at the Imperial Hotel in Tokyo, where he cleared tables after meals—often for American officers who were housed at the hotel. He would eat the leftovers when no one was looking. One day, he was caught by his boss, the head chef, eating from a half-full plate he had cleared. The screaming and commotion attracted the attention of an American woman in the dining room who wanted to know what had happened. Her husband also took interest. My friend explained that he was eating because he was hungry—he did not have enough to eat despite the job. The woman's husband promised my friend that he would never go hungry again. And that is how my friend came to personally know General Douglas MacArthur and his wife.

What motivates and drives people when their basic needs are unmet tend to be things like more money, more food, and better shelter. However, once basic needs are met, what drives people is different. Ambitions change. In the Japanese age of Peace and Prosperity, many Japanese people are looking for much more than just an iron rice bowl. They are willing to take risks for the upside reward of achieving their ambitions, as the downside risk of not having enough food to eat is remote. Those are the people that you want in your company—not the ones who are looking for the iron rice bowl.

If your company's practice is to offer a cast iron rice bowl, you will attract only people with a mentality of scarcity, who are willing to exchange ambition for security. Those are not people who will empower your company to grow and change, but rather cause it to calcify. Your company can still be good, but it will never likely be great. If conditions change too rapidly, your company may be incapable of adapting rapidly enough to thrive or even survive, as we have seen happen to many once-successful Japanese firms. The iron rice bowl also drives away the most ambitious, least fearful people with the greatest talent and value to offer. Break the iron rice bowl. You will drive away the mediocre and attract the excellent. If you keep the iron rice bowl, the mediocre will collect in your business like stagnant water in low-lying land, while the excellent flee to higher ground.

Heisei is about restoring a real peace and prosperity to Japan that matches with the conditions of this time and age. Be an agent of the *Heisei Restoration*.

Not Lifetime Employment—Lifetime Employable

One of my Japanese company clients, a Tokyo-based firm, employs a number of non-Japanese staff, including several Americans, a Russian, a person from China (whom I had introduced and they hired), and a person from Thailand. The company was founded just after the Second World War and grew with Japan's economic miracle. It is still family-owned and run. Its current leaders are internationally minded and forward thinking, even though the company continues some traditional Japanese employment practices, among which is lifetime employment.

However, lifetime employment is not for everyone. New-hires may choose between limited term contracts and unlimited term contracts, the latter being code for "lifetime." Once I asked the company's HR director what percentage of people opt for which type of contract. He told me, "Pretty much everyone opts for the unlimited term contract, that is to say lifetime employment, except for the non-Japanese employees. They have all chosen the limited term contract."

This made me suspicious that the company had established a tacit two-class system for Japanese and non-Japanese, where in reality it offered lifetime employment only to the Japanese. I talked with one of the more senior mid-level non-Japanese managers who had been with the company for a decade. He explained to me, "I opted for the limited term contract because the salary is significantly higher and I get a constant base salary every month, as opposed to the unlimited term contract employees who have a lower salary, and have to wait six months every year to collect their bonus pay."

A note for those not familiar with Japan's bonus system: In Japan, about five-months' worth of salary is paid out in July and December "bonuses." These are not extra pay at the discretion of management for good performance. Rather, these bonuses are mostly fixed. They are effectively deferred salary. In extreme economic circumstances, a company can also cut bonuses more easily than salary if necessary.

When I asked this non-Japanese manager if he was not concerned about his job security, he said, "No." He is confident in the value he provides to the company, and does not worry about his contract not being renewed. In any case if it weren't renewed, he was confident that he could find another job. He is good at what he does and has developed good contacts in the industry.

"Lifetime employment is really meaningless. For such a supposed guarantee, you pay through the nose. In my case, I make more money than a lot of people senior to me, and I'd have to be kind of crazy to opt for the unlimited duration contract. And in any case, I want to keep my options open. Maybe I won't want to work here my entire life. I don't want my managers to simply assume that I do."

This manager is currently the top-performing sales director in the company, and he is on a limited term contract!

A Japanese manager from a big Japanese bank approached me personally to ask for advice. He is a very bright guy, having graduated from a top university in Japan. He has an MBA from a famous American school, and had just returned from a five-year assignment in London. His English is impeccable. He was concerned because he was coming to an age where the bank typically decides whether to put a manager on a track for senior executive management, or otherwise sideline him, ultimately transferring him to some position in a rural outpost—the dumping ground for those who simply don't make the grade. He was fretting that he might end up being sidelined, though I don't believe he really had cause to think so. In any case, he asked me what I thought he should do.

ME	Do you like working at the bank?
THE MANAGER	No, I hate it, and have for a long time.
ME	Do you think you will like working there if you ended up on the senior executive track?
THE MANAGER	No. I doubt it.
ME	OK. So quit.
THE MANAGER	But why?
ME	You hate working there now. You don't like either option working there in the future, whether you make the cut or not.
THE MANAGER	Where would I go? What would I do?

ME   You're a smart guy. You have a track record of suc-
                  cess. You have an MBA from a top school. You've
                  worked in one of the top banks in Japan. You speak
                  impeccable English and have excellent overseas
                  business experience. A lot companies would be
                  interested in someone like you.
THE MANAGER   You mean foreign companies, right?
ME   Yes. You would have far more opportunity in foreign
                  companies and the pay is a lot better.
THE MANAGER   Yes, but foreign companies lay people off. I have
                  lifetime employment with the bank.
ME   Sure, but even if you were laid off from a foreign
                  company, how long do you think you would remain
                  unemployed? You're very talented, and you would find
                  another position quickly. You believe that, don't you?
THE MANAGER   No. It's too risky. I need to stay with the bank.

This is a highly capable manager, with highly irrational fears that drive
his behaviors and decisions. Despite his abilities, how do you think
he behaves at the bank? If he is miserable in his job, do you think he
can be a top performer, even if he makes it onto the executive management track? I have never known unhappy employees to be stellar
performers.

The same manager later came to me for advice on a strategy problem
at the bank. He was part of a strategic planning department. Strategy was
failing, and the leadership was convinced that the cause had to do with
the strategy development methodology. The manager and his team had
been tasked with coming up with changes to the methodology to fix the
problem.

ME   All strategy development starts with deciding the
                  future outcomes you desire. Once those are clear,
                  you develop strategy by working backwards. I know
                  that the methodology you use starts with desired
                  outcomes. Are you making desired outcomes clear?
THE MANAGER   Well, no. The desired business outcomes are never
                  made clear by our executive management. They are
                  always deliberately ambiguous and vague about
                  objectives apart from financial targets.

ME   Well, there's your problem. You need to talk with the executive leadership about clarity of business objectives first. Perhaps you could help them develop the clarity.

THE MANAGER   I know that lack of clarity of the objectives is the problem, but I couldn't possibly tell the executives that! I need to find a solution that implicates weaknesses in the methodology as the cause because that's what my bosses want to hear. Think! I can't suggest to the leadership to change the way they go about developing strategic objectives!

This manager has the ability to be of tremendous help to the bank's business and to the bank's leadership, but he is too timorous to do so. He fears putting his career at risk if he talks with his managers about the real cause of the problem. His staff know the real cause of the problem as well, but do you think the staff will communicate that to the senior leadership while their current manager is in charge?

What's the point of employing highly intelligent and capable managers if they are too afraid to use their capabilities for fear of offending a superior? To make matters worse, a fearful mid-level manager will project his fear onto all staff below him, who will mimic the behavior even though they may not be fearful themselves—a true refraction layer.

I can't say for sure whether this manager's fear is justified or not, but I think it is probably not. If you as a leader wanted to improve the success of your business, and a trusted manager came and told you how you could do it and was there to support you through it, wouldn't you want that? Would you want to keep that manager close to you? Wouldn't you want to ensure that they get onto the executive track?

While this manager is so concerned about guaranteeing his lifetime employment, he is neglecting opportunities to make himself lifetime employable!

When I have talked with CEOs about abandoning the lifetime employment system, I am often told, "We couldn't possibly do that! We have a hard enough time attracting the best candidates as it is. Without lifetime employment, who would want to work for us?"

People who are confident in their own capabilities, for starters. Sure, you can attract people to your business with the offer of lifetime employment, but are these really the kind of people you want working for you?

Lifetime employment attracts the timorous. It is a system that appeals to people who prefer limited downside risk, no matter how infinitesimal, rather than maximizing upside reward, no matter how reasonably achievable. Lifetime employment creates an attitude of entitlement, and an expectation of paternalism on the part of the company. You would think that the guarantee of not ever being laid off would encourage people to take greater risks for greater reward, but I have never seen this to be the case. To the contrary, the protection makes people slow and reactive. They coast. They develop a hypersensitivity to remote risk with negligible impact if ever realized.

If you want the kind of managers who will perform for your business, are open to change, are willing to give their advice and opinions on improving the business even when that advice is contrary to the blowing winds, and are driven to do better, do away with lifetime employment if your business has it, and never implement a policy of lifetime employment if there is none to begin with.

Pro Forma Meritocracies and Other Sesame Grinders

Old habits die hard. Seniority-based promotion was once the hallmark of the Japanese company and enshrined in official policy. Like lifetime employment, companies are turning away from the policy. However, the practice continues. For example, I suggested to the leader of a client company of mine to promote a star-performing manager to a division head position. His response was that he could not possibly do that because it would mean that he would be at the same level as managers who had served years longer than he had. This is a company that had supposedly abandoned seniority-based promotion. I asked why not.

"The other managers at his level would feel bad," the leader claimed. None of the other managers were performing as well as the junior star.

"Why are you worried about making your mediocre performers feel bad by promoting your stars? I would be far more concerned about alienating your star performers because you don't recognize their achievements, while you coddle the mediocre."

The efforts to reform seniority-based promotion in many companies with which I work are more often pro forma than proactive. For those accustomed to a seniority-based system, merit-based promotion is easy when it happens to correspond more or less with an employee's seniority. It's when it does not that makes people uncomfortable, like in the example above—the junior manager was so good that he was certainly ready for the position, even though he was 15 years younger than would-be peers at that level.

The opposite case can also make people uncomfortable—a senior employee who doesn't make the grade and is held back will at some point find their manager is younger, less senior then they are in the company, or is otherwise a peer in terms of length of service. It is in these cases when a company is tested, as is the resolve of its leadership. Managers sometimes decide simply to push the employee up rather than confronting that awkward and imbalanced situation. However, doing so is a disservice to the business and to the junior staff whom the manager will now lead.

The pressure on Japanese companies to end the system of seniority-based promotion comes not just from economic imperative. As Japanese companies become more international in mergers and acquisitions overseas, maintaining a two-class system for employees—a Japanese one which is seniority-based and a non-Japanese one which is merit-based—simply becomes untenable. A large global foreign client firm of mine acquired a Japanese business. As overseas employees began to be transferred to Japan, working alongside Japanese managers, discrepancies in attitude became immediately apparent—their Japanese counterparts appeared slow-moving and unconcerned, with little sense of business urgency, and there was an alarming lack of business acumen among the managers.

One foreign manager who was given a department full of Japanese employees from the acquired business remarked, "I have to learn a whole new way of talking one-to-one with my staff as I mentor them. In other countries, it is through career discussion that I have been able to motivate and influence staff. Yet in Japan, none of my staff seem to have any interest in managing their careers! They simply have never had to in the past, because advancement was based primarily on putting in the time!"

The company's Japan CEO remarked that there is effectively a two-class system: "People from the acquired company working at equivalent levels as staff originally from our business are paid nearly two times more salary in most cases, sometimes more, for more or less the same job. How do we justify that? If I brought their pay up to our levels, I would have to make major cuts in staff to remain profitable!"

Seniority-based promotion and lifetime employment feed off each other. There is less pressure to make an employee immediately productive because the view of their contribution to the company extends out decades until retirement. In one company with which I work, it is three years before a new-hire salesperson is considered capable of independent customer calls. Granted, for complex technical products there is a learning curve, as well as a learning curve in selling in general—but three years?

It is possible to map out a new-hire's career progression with relative accuracy. There are only slight variations and some wiggle room in timing. It is only at very senior levels where an employee may be viewed as a candidate for an executive-level position, or otherwise take a track in which they may coast until retirement.

Seniority-based promotion has also influenced the way a person's capability is judged in many organizations—essentially, capability and years of service become equivalent in the thinking of people who are part of this seniority-based system, as opposed to judging capability based on individual results. Seniority-based promotion homogenizes people's talents—it is inconceivable that a person in his twenties may be more capable than a person in his forties at the same task.

The seniority-based promotion system encourages setting the bar relatively low for promotion, as all need to be able to pass it with few exceptions. Some may take longer than others by one or two years, but for the most part, all make it.

In people's minds, time and effort are considered valuable in themselves—without regard for productivity. This leads to a sense of entitlement for putting in time. Once that becomes acceptable, remunerated overtime without productivity becomes acceptable as well. In many companies in Japan, overtime simply becomes part of the standard workday, and some people rely on the overtime pay for their income, even though there is very little additional productivity for the time spent.

Even in cases where overtime is not remunerated, many managers habitually stay late. The European CEO of a non-Japanese firm in Tokyo tried to eliminate excessive, habitual overtime without productivity. Director-level managers, who are not remunerated for overtime, vehemently opposed the plan, even though financially it would not hurt them at all. There are a number of reasons for their motivation to oppose the plan, one of which is equating time put in with the value of one's contribution to the business. Effectively, they viewed the attempt at cutting time as a deliberate attempt to reduce their individual value and contribution to the business. They viewed that as a threat to their jobs.

When your senior- to mid-level managers view themselves as entitled to their positions regardless of performance, staff below them will begin to think in the same way. Putting in time will take priority over producing results. They will buy into the system that works for their immediate managers, mimic them, and become like them when they are promoted themselves.

Most CEOs with whom I work are convinced that a seniority-based promotion system, whether policy or practice, does not benefit the company. The question is how to switch to a merit-based system when a seniority-based system is well-entrenched.

I frequently see reform-minded leaders decide to start with the most junior generation, as they have given up on the more senior ones. They attempt to mandate merit-based evaluations and reward via reforming systems in HR; for example, by revising the bi-annual individual review form to be used by managers when evaluating staff. While well-intentioned, this simply does not work, as the managers are being asked to hold their staff accountable for performance in ways that they themselves are not held accountable by their own managers. Managers who achieve their own business objectives and promotion via the success of the people they manage have strong motivation to coach their staff and cultivate staff capabilities. They want their people to perform well and will hold them accountable for doing so because that is how they get ahead. However, in a system in which a manager gets ahead despite the performance of the staff they lead, where is the motivation to coach, cultivate, and hold staff accountable for performance?

In companies with seniority-based promotion, I see managers become passive toward their staff. They don't coach, and rarely hold staff accountable for results. For poorly performing staff, they become apologists. For example, they say things such as, "Yes, but he works really hard and puts in a lot of time." Or "But she is a really nice person and customers like her."

Why shouldn't they be apologists? Coaching staff is hard, and holding people accountable can lead to uncomfortable confrontation. If they are still working within a seniority-based system, they have nothing to gain personally by implementing a merit-based system for the next generation. When it comes to the HR-mandated reviews, whether a merit-based component has been added or not, they simply go through the motions without putting it into practice.

Without addressing seniority-based promotion at senior levels of management, it is futile addressing it at more junior levels. The senior level is the refraction layer. If you are going to end seniority-based promotion in your company, it has to be done for everyone.

Windowsill Gangs

Lifetime employment and seniority-based promotion creates a dilemma. What do you do with managers who simply don't meet expectations, despite all efforts and support? They become part of a group of managers notoriously dubbed "the windowsill gang," or *madogiwazoku*. The windowsill is a metaphor for the sideline. As the story goes, a non-performing manager is given no particular responsibilities or work, just a seat by the window so they do not get entirely bored as they while away their day, reading Japanese *manga*, or comic books, looking up occasionally to peer out the window wistfully at the passing world, all the while continuing to collect their salary until retirement.

In reality, I have never seen a non-performing manager placed by the window, but windowsill gang members do exist. Rather than giving them no work and allowing them to work their way through stacks of comic books, *madogiwazoku* are more typically given a job of low or no importance, and sometimes even given staff to help them achieve—uh, well—I'm not really quite sure what. They are not infrequently transferred from the head office in Tokyo to some smaller regional office that requires some minimal caretaking that won't challenge them too much, or threaten the business much should they underperform.

I have witnessed windowsill gang members in companies that claim to have transitioned away from lifetime employment and seniority-based leadership. In this case, while policy may have changed, practice remains. I have seen this both in Japanese and non-Japanese firms in Japan.

For example, I discussed in the first chapter how the leader of a Japanese company, one of my clients, was ready to "windowsill" a non-performing manager. Despite all efforts, the manager just did not improve. Five years away from retirement, the leader thought it best to give him a non-challenging bit of work of little consequence, along with an impressive-sounding title, so as not to cause the manager to lose face. I recount below how my conversation with the leader went, to illustrate the leader's thinking:

LEADER	I could make him head of strategic planning, and put him in charge of the strategic planning team.
ME	You have some very talented and motivated junior staff on that team. If you put this manager in charge of them, they will wither. Some may even leave the company in search of opportunities where they can grow. And in any case, the idea that your strategic planning department is of so little consequence that you would be happy to give it over to an incompetent manager is a problem in itself. We ought to address that.
LEADER	Well, I can't just fire him like you do in America. We have labor laws here!
ME	I don't think you should just fire him. If he is not working out, that is the company's fault, not his. You made the decision to hire him. If you are going to remove him, do it humanely. Take responsibility.
LEADER	How?
ME	For example, offer him an early retirement package. If you offered to pay him five-years' worth of salary in a lump sum and allowed him to keep his pension, I think he would jump at the chance, and you would part on good terms. He would have the freedom to pursue whatever he wants—retire, find another job, start a business, etc. He would be far better off, and so would you.
LEADER	Just pay him to leave—for nothing?
ME	You were going to pay him for nothing anyway. You don't need a sidelined manager moping about your company, eating up overhead, and poisoning the atmosphere.

LEADER   Ok. I get that.

ME   You especially don't want to give him staff! That would make his staff unproductive as well, and miserable under an incompetent boss. You would stifle their growth, and perhaps lose the talented ones to competitors. Removing this manager may sound harsh, but it is the right thing to do for all involved.

LEADER   Ok. But if I do this, won't other managers be demoralized? Some might even quit.

ME   Unlikely. The mediocre and poor performers are always concerned they will not be able to find new work. They won't quit, even though you might rather they did.

LEADER   I believe that is correct.

ME   As for demotivating staff, I doubt it. A top performer will never be demotivated seeing a non-performer removed. Non-performers might experience a shock, though. In some cases, they may feel that they are next and pre-empt you by resigning. Let them.

LEADER   But then I will have an empty role to fill!

ME   There is no scarcity of talented managers if you treat your people right. Far better to go through the effort of finding and keeping talented people in management positions than to tolerate an empty suit as a placeholder because you are afraid to let him go.

LEADER   Ok. I need to think about this.

Windowsilling non-productive managers is not only financially costly, but also fundamentally unethical. You are not doing an employee any favors by keeping them in a job to which they are unsuited. It limits the employee's future potential, makes them miserable, and can lead to depression. You need to let the employee go so they can find their own way to fulfillment.

It is also unethical toward your other staff. Having a miserable, unproductive employee hanging about detracts from the energy and enthusiasm of other people. It eats up resources, limiting opportunities for the talented and deserving.

The most egregious cases of windowsilling occur when the non-productive manager is given staff. Windowsilled managers with staff become refraction layers. The staff are then made unproductive themselves, and their potential for growth is hampered. I have never found happy staff working under a windowsilled manager, and never see good customer service from a company whose staff are unhappy.

Are there windowsill gangs in your company? Does windowsilling happen in your company, if not by policy then by practice? If so, you must end the practice. You may encounter resistance from your other managers and even from your HR director. You need to end windowsilling anyway. It's best for your business financially, best for managers who are not working out, best for other staff, and best for your customers. Ending windowsilling is not only best for your business, it is the ethical thing to do.

You can find additional resources on the topics discussed in this chapter and more at *www.relansa.co.jp.*

CHAPTER 6

From Process-Driven Thinking to Thinking-Driven Process

Too many companies in Japan are dominated by process-driven thinking, when what is really needed is thinking-driven processes. Process-driven thinking is all about adherence—following a process meticulously and consistently—something that the Japanese feel that they are particularly good at. Thinking-driven processes on the other hand are all about contingence—what you do is contingent upon the situation, and will naturally vary. Calcified processes form refraction layers in mid-level management, because they are resistant to change. When process is contingent upon need, mid-level management is adaptable to change.

Companies have myriad managers obsessed with doing things right, while CEOs wish that far more of them would be more concerned with doing the right things. The latter is harder as there is no work more physically demanding than thinking. And there is risk. In process-driven thinking, individual success or failure is based on adherence to form regardless of outcome. In thinking-driven process, success or failure is based on outcome—form is flexible.

This chapter discusses a critical transition in mindset and behaviors that mid-level managers must achieve to become partners in change rather than reactionaries who impede it. The chapter provides practical tools for inculcating the mindset and desired behaviors in mid-level managers.

Shifting to Outcome-Orientation, not just "Gambarimasu!"

The Japanese have a curious expression. *Gambarimasu* literally means to put in effort, to do one's best, to give it a go. However, the way the expression is used differs from how and when the translated expressions are used in English.

For example, if you ask the members of a high school football team in the US whether or not they will win the next match, almost invariably the team will say, "We will win!" In Japan, a similar team would say, *"Gambarimasu!"*, which is not quite the same. *Gambarimasu* puts the emphasis on the process and the effort, whereas "We will win!" puts the emphasis on the desired result. *Gambarimasu* is a hedge against failure—perhaps even *anticipated* failure, whereas "We will win!" allows no room for self-doubt.

The attitude extends into professional life. For example, when a leader asks a manager whether they will achieve their targets, the answer is often *Gambarimasu!* in Japanese, or if asked in English, the response might be one of the following:

* I will do my best.
* I will try.
* I will put in the effort.

Such non-committal answers don't usually sit well with a non-Japanese manager, who would rather hear a resounding yes, or at least what is being done to mitigate risk of failure if there are concerns. Non-Japanese managers tend to be less concerned with process and more concerned with the outcome to be achieved.

Language is often a reflection of values and thinking, and at the same time, language can influence values and thinking. In business, I have found the Japanese tend to be process-oriented as opposed to outcome-oriented, as the use of *Gambarimasu!* might suggest. For example, of a non-performing manager or staff person, I have not infrequently heard a business leader say, "Yes, but he does a really good job and works really hard." Lifetime employment and seniority-based promotion systems reinforce process-orientation because individual results make little difference.

Process-orientation leads to calcification of ways of doing things, as there is a constant emphasis on optimizing a process that may be achieving suboptimal results. Outcome-orientation tends to encourage flexibility— if a process is not achieving the desired outcome, change the process.

The best way to create a shift toward outcome-orientation is to change the way you talk about process—always discuss process in the context of desired business goals. For example, an executive at a client company was struggling with several managers under him who resisted doing their jobs in a new way. They argued with him about process— insisting the current way was best. I advised him to say the following in this conversation:

"We have three strategic imperatives this year—increase pace of new store opening, reduce costs of fitting new retail space while maintaining branding requirements, and reduce lead time on new projects. How is what you are suggesting going to help us achieve those three imperatives?"

To another executive fed up with the expressions of *Gambarimasu,* I advised not to just accept that, or simply demand commitment to results, i.e: "I want you to hit the targets, not just try!" Instead, say the following, "I know you'll put in the effort, but I would like to know what you intend to change about the way you are doing things now that will achieve the more challenging results? After all, we cannot hit our targets by simply doing more of the same thing or just doing it a bit better."

In my experience, when managers report progress to a superior, many have the tendency to give a relatively long-winded background on what they did and then their conclusions from the experiences and/or the results. A lot words are devoted to background, and very few devoted to the results, much less a discussion about what was learned and how to improve. When getting reports from managers, insist that they present results first, and then have a discussion on what was learned—what worked, what didn't, reasons why for both what worked and what didn't, and what they plan to change in terms of process if anything to improve future results. Insist that they don't need to report background or detail of what they did. Tell them that if you need background to understand, you will ask for it.

For example, a verbal report might start like this: "Last quarter we were able to open more stores than we had planned, exceeding our target by 20 percent. However, fitting costs went up by about 10 percent. Now, I am going to talk about what worked, what didn't work, and why. After that I will talk about what we plan to change based on what we learned. I want to leave some time for discussion, and if you need clarification on anything, just ask."

Earlier I wrote that language reflects thinking. At the same time, change in language can drive change in thinking. By insisting on communicating in a way that makes desired outcomes the primary drivers of any discussion of process, you effectively require a change in thinking that puts results first. If you can effect change in thinking, change in behavior follows. It is in this way that you can eliminate *Gambarimasu* thinking and attitudes. This is the first step in achieving a shift to thinking-driven process away from process-driven thinking.

I am a Cat, and Curiosity Does Not Kill Me

Like the cat, curiously observing human society around him in Natsume Soseki's novel, *I am a Cat,* thinking-driven process requires a curiosity about the world. In many organizations, there is a curious lack of curiosity regarding the way things are done and the world outside the business. At the root of curiosity is aberration—something that deviates from the norm or what might be expected. When we observe something unexpected, the curious ask *why?* and try to discover the answer. The curious also have the ability to imagine a future reality, and the proactive then set about creating it.

Note that an aberration need not be negative. You need curiosity about the positive too. So, for example, a first-time customer from an industry in which one of my client companies had never been active, came to enquire about one of the chemical products my client manufactures. The manager whose team fielded the enquiry had enough acumen to sense the value of the product to this new customer. A non-commodity product developed with proprietary technology, the manager quoted a price ten times higher than typically quoted in the industry in which the company normally sells, and the customer bought it! Happily, in fact. The product was that valuable to the customer for whatever the intended purpose was.

What the manager did was a deviation from his company's standard process, which is to price products using cost-plus—adding a standard fixed margin based on the cost of manufacturing the product, regardless of the product. Many managers would have simply followed the process without thinking and undercharged for the product. That's process-driven thinking. It creates rigidity that inevitably results in lost opportunity. Without an understanding of what the customer values, pricing according to cost-plus methods will inevitably price the product too low, and you leave money on the table, or too high, and you lose the sale! Curiosity about the customer's business from the customer's perspective, not your own business's perspective, helps you understand what customers value, and that always leads to better business results for both you and the customer!

For the manager who took a chance and deviated from the process, this was a nice win. Good on him for charging based on a sense of value to the customer. That's thinking-driven process—the manager thought of the desired outcome, and changed the process to the benefit of the business.

So, for thinking-driven process in terms of this single action, I give the manager a grade of A. However, in terms of curiosity, I give him D−. Why, you ask? Good. I'm glad you're curious about that! The manager pursued this matter no further after the win. He assumed it was a lucky one-off transaction. Yes, he doesn't actually *know* whether it was just a one-off. Curiosity would have led me to ask a lot of questions, such as:

What is the customer using this product for?
If it is an ingredient for product, what product is it?
Are there other companies in this industry that have a need for the same product?
What other uses for this product might we not be aware of?
Could I have charged more for this product?

Species evolve in spurts. What takes an animal species to the next level is some sort of aberration—either an aberration in their development, such as one beetle being born with wings, or an aberration in the environment, such as glaciers receding to reveal vast plains. It is aberrations that take a species forward, and it is aberrations that propel businesses to the next level.

The irony is that the practice of management tends to work against aberration. Managers use techniques to maintain consistency and achieve predictable planned results, often on a quarterly basis. Aberration is typically viewed as a bad thing rather than good. So it gets stifled or ignored.

It is not necessary to rely on serendipity for the good aberrations that may come your way. Build aberration into your business. Give managers latitude to change processes on the fly. Accept that, with that, there will be some losses but also a lot of wins. I also recommend setting aside a certain amount of time weekly to depart from regular routine. For example, for a sales team, set aside time specifically *not to sell*. Yes, you read that right. Instead of selling, visit customers and prospects and ask questions about new products the company is considering for development, how their businesses are dealing with different developments in the market, what they would change if they could, or what would be their dream product and why, and what are their strategic priorities for the coming year.

The key to making this effective is to embed it within the routine. As with innovation, departure from routine is too often deemed to be discretionary on the part of the employee. Left to their own devices, employees, no matter how good, are unlikely to exploit the opportunity being given to them. Not that departure from routine should be institutionalized and stymied by bureaucratic processes, and neither should innovation. However, a one-off visit, or a one-off project, will almost never yield the required results. What is needed is a direction, like each week you are tasked with visiting a customer and prospect and asking their views on new products under development. Curiosity is like a muscle. If you don't use it, or exercise it, it atrophies. Start using it, and it becomes stronger. Do the motions, and they become part of muscle memory. Just doing these types of activities regularly encourages curiosity to become a natural part of the way one works. Insufficient curiosity leads to lost opportunity, and sometimes those opportunities could be significant enough to take company performance to a whole new level, which is the subject of the next section.

Innovation, Shminnovation

There are two kinds of business performance improvement—innovation and *shminnovation*. *Shminnovation* is simply about doing things better, whereas innovation is about doing better things. Both are good for business, but it is innovation that allows a business to grow to a new level. The two, however, are often confused. What is really just optimization, is often passed off as innovation. My grandmother would have dismissively called that *shminnovation*.

So, for example, improving a contract close rate by changing the way sales teams talk with customers and prospects by way of modifying the method and techniques of that interaction is optimization. Depending on the starting point, it can have a dramatic effect on revenues. For example, a 40 percent close rate that doubles to 80 percent could double revenues. Yet, this is really optimization of sales processes. The company is still selling the same products to the same addressable market, but has optimized its methods. The possible performance increase diminishes as it approaches the limit of the addressable market. You can go from 80 percent to 90 percent and then to 95 percent and so on. So the curve looks like Figure 6.1.

However, let's say you come up with a whole new application for an existing product in an industry the business had never considered before, where the value of the product is much higher, allowing you to charge more and reap greater profits, like in the example in the previous section. That takes business performance to a whole new level. That's innovation. The curve looks different, like Figure 6.2.

Innovation creates a new standard of performance that is sustainable into the future. Innovation is always accompanied by obsolescence of

FIGURE 6.1 Optimization curve

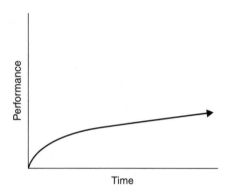

FIGURE 6.2 Innovation curve

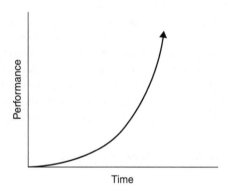

some type. So, for example, with the discovery of the more lucrative market for the proprietary chemical product in a different industry, selling it in the former industry may become an obsolete practice if customers there cannot bear the price increase.

Businesses tend to go through short periods of bursts of innovation followed by longer periods of optimization. The curve looks something like Figure 6.3.

The problem is that markets, economies, and competitors are in constant flux. Innovation has a use-by date. Eventually it expires. So, for example, Blackberry mobile phones were a dramatic innovation that

FIGURE 6.3 Bursts of innovation and periods of optimization

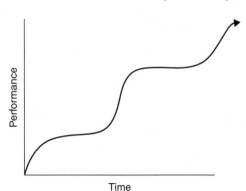

changed the way people did business. People became more mobile. That's the short burst. Research in Motion, the company behind the Blackberry, continued to optimize the device and services, but there was no further dramatic innovation. The iPhone, and then smartphones very similar to the iPhone, ended Blackberry's run. The use-by date had been reached. So, for every innovation, there is a limit somewhere out into the future. It is never possible to know how far out into the future, but it is a certainty that is there. Your innovation will ultimately be made obsolete by someone else's or one of your own. The curve looks like Figure 6.4.

FIGURE 6.4 Shiminnovation limit

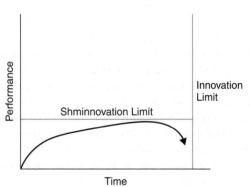

Perpetual *shminnovation* ultimately leads to failure. In some industries, innovation has a shorter life-cycle than others; but, make no mistake, a business cannot grow and succeed into the future without regular innovation.

The Shminnovation Gap

I have never met a CEO who doesn't want more innovation and innovative thinking in their business, and most businesses achieve regular business improvement to some degree. The problem is that when a leader demands innovation, what is often delivered is optimization. While positive, *shminnovation* leaves a leader with a feeling of want—that the business should be on the steeply rising innovation curve, but is in fact on the optimization curve. I call this the *shminnovation* gap (see Figure 6.5).

For example, one CEO of a company in Japan told me, "My people are just not innovative enough. They rarely come up with new product ideas, and when they do, it's mostly a small variation on an existing product or a combination of existing products. We used to come up with breakthrough products regularly. We seem to have lost that capability."

Whenever a CEO tells me people in the company are not innovative enough—that there is a dearth of ideas for new products, processes, technologies, and ways of selling—I always ask, "What is your process for generating ideas?"

Innovation is not the problem. It's ideation.

FIGURE 6.5 Shminnovation gap

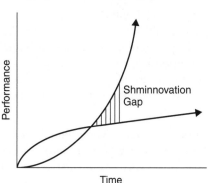

Most companies have some sort of product development process—some are more formal than others. However, the root cause of a lack of innovation is rarely in the product development process. Rather it is what happens before product development that really counts. This is ideation, i.e. the process for developing ideas. The rate of innovation is always limited by the quantity and quality of ideas being funneled into it. There are an infinite number of ideas floating around in the ether of the universe, invisible like dark matter. They are looking for a human host to bring them to the visible side of the universe. A host has to be open to ideas in order to attract an idea. If a human host doesn't appear open to ideas, because of lack of curiosity or because of fear, the idea moves on and looks for a more attractive host, and usually finds one—with a current or future competitor to your business!

Entreating your people to generate more ideas is absolutely futile. People do not generate ideas simply because they are asked to do so. Ideas are attracted to people who are open to them. Ideation is not about making ideas attractive to your people. Ideation is about making your people attractive to ideas.

There is someone for everyone—so the saying goes. Everyone is capable of being attractive to ideas. It is in our nature. We all emit a kind of ethereal pheromone to which ideas are drawn. Some people do so naturally, and these are the innovation "geniuses" of which many are jealous. However, it is not genius that attracts ideas so much as it is a mindset that makes people attractive to ideas. That mindset includes a healthy curiosity and *courage.*

Why courage? People have all sorts of irrational fears related to ideas:

- What if it doesn't work? I will be blamed.
- What if everyone thinks it's stupid? People will look down on me.
- What if I ended up volunteering myself to be individually responsible for making the idea a reality, simply because I proposed it? I may end up having to do more work for a futile cause.
- What if my idea is in conflict with what my boss thinks? I will be penalized.

Shifting to an idea-honey mindset, where one does not necessarily exist, can be achieved through turning ideation into a process. Ideation must be driven by a leader to be successful—first as a CEO with their senior leadership, and then extended to mid-level leaders on down. In this way, you can close the *shminnovation* gap. The key to closing the *shminnovation* gap is ideation.

Here are seven guiding principles for successful ideation.

Schedule Ideation Regularly; Don't Wait for Serendipity

In most companies in which the CEO tells me there is a dearth of innovation, no regular ideation sessions are held. There may be marketing meetings where new ideas are discussed, and there may be a practice to be open to new ideas during meetings—indeed it may even figure on the agenda—but there is nothing in terms of a time set aside that is dedicated to nothing but ideas.

In the same way, if you want to write a book, an article, a dissertation, etc., you don't wait for ideas to come to you before you write. You schedule time to write and just write, attracting ideas and entreating them to come. You don't worry about quality, or what other people might think of your writing. You go for volume. Ideation is the same. Ideation sessions can be held in workshop format. You may hold them with or without asking people to prepare. They can be as short as one hour, or could last over several days. The key is for them to happen on a regular basis and for there to be a clear infrastructure that supports those ideas that are deemed to be ones with potential. Without this, the ideation sessions are pointless and can be viewed as counterproductive by staff.

Ask Provocative Questions

There are three fundamental types of business innovation: product, process, and customer. Provocative questions will always be about one or more of these. Below are some examples of provocative questions that spur thinking that, in turn, attracts ideas.

Product
1. For which products and services are we undercharging?
2. What uses might there be for our products in other industries?
3. How can we provide increased value of our products, raise our prices, and increase our sales at the same time?

4. If we were to cut half our product line-up, which products would we cut and why?

5. What would an impulse-buy, premium-priced product of ours look like?

Process

1. Who else might be buying our products if we changed the way we sell?

2. What capabilities might we internalize, and which should we out-source to shorten go-to-market lead time on new products?

3. If we had a magic wand, what changes would we make to shorten lead times?

4. Which departments do we rely on in collaboration to achieve our strategic results? How do we rely on them? When does that collaboration fail and why?

5. What change in the way we sell and deliver our product would make it more valuable to the customer?

Customer

1. Which prospects are choosing not to buy from us, about whom we have no data because there was no transaction, and why did they not buy?

2. To which customers does our level of quality make a difference and why, and to which customers would quality at a lower standard be acceptable?

3. What would make a current customer want more of what we have to sell?

4. Which customers are not buying from us because access to us is too difficult?

5. What is the value to the customer of the problem our product helps solve? Are we charging enough for the value we provide?

6. How can we increase value and charge more?

Use these questions to start a discussion. Follow up with more provoca-tive questions on a topic. Ideas will start to flow. Be sure that someone is documenting the ideas for later review.

You May Say "Yes, and ..." You May Never Say "Yes, but ..."

In ideation, there is a tendency to want to analyze and critique an idea as soon as it is brought up. As a rule, don't allow this. Analysis and critique will come later. Participants may say, "Yes, and ..." and add to an idea, but never "Yes, but ..." to critique it.

A person's worst critic is often themself, so this rule has to apply to themself too. Here the problem is that no one is privy to the private critique going on in another person's head. We often have ideas and then immediately critique and dismiss them before we ever share them with others. In ideation, participants must resist the tendency to self-edit to bring about maximum effectiveness.

What is needed is a clear validation process.

All Ideas Are Valid Until Invalidated Through Process, Not Just By Way of Someone's Opinion

A CEO of a client company once complained to me, "When sales people in my company have an idea for a new product, it often gets strangled in the crib. Internal 'experts' immediately look for and find reasons why something won't work—our suppliers won't help us, technically it is infeasible, it will cannibalize our other products, etc.—and discussions end. It is only later that I hear about some of these ideas and think they might have had legs if we had worked at resolving concerns rather than rejecting the ideas out-of-hand."

Make sure there is a validation process, and criteria for progressing an idea, so no idea is summarily nixed by a powerful naysayer.

The Process of Validation Must Be Transparent to Everyone

At one client company, I surveyed the viewpoints of a wide spectrum of people regarding coming up with new ideas innovation. Many of the people I interviewed said they had ideas and suggested them, but these were never taken up, and they never knew why not. They were not sure whether the idea had even been passed on. Their suggestions simply went into a black hole. After a while, many people simply stopped making suggestions. Why bother?

A process is not enough. If you want to keep people motivated in coming up with ideas, they must be able to see the results of their efforts. People are much more interested in seeing that their ideas have had a fair go at making it, even if they are ultimately rejected. In my experience, there is nothing more demotivating to the creation of ideas than if they disappear the minute they are vocalized. When there is no transparency, even if a good process is in place, an idea that just disappears is the same as an idea that was ignored or rejected out-of-hand. This is deeply counterproductive and will always limit the ideas that are being put forward internally.

Involve People from All Parts of the Organization

Ideas don't care about the rank, age, or education of a host. In ideation sessions, particularly in Japan, leaders should always speak last.

This is important because a good idea may originate with someone who may not be willing to speak when senior decision makers have the floor. For example, Docomo's highly successful iMode service, which led early mobile communication for years, was the brainchild of a female office worker in the company.

Ideas can be attracted to anyone, and are particularly attracted to a diverse group of people engaged in lively, positive discussion.

Most Good Ideas Don't Work, and That's OK

Ideation is far more about the quantity of ideas, not coming up with the "right" idea. In ideation, success is measured in volume.

If you feel your business is suffering from a *shminnovation* gap, focus on improving ideation at mid-level layers of management.

Constructive Disharmony—the *Wa* of Confrontation

Thinking-driven processes inevitably lead to confrontation. Anytime someone says, "I think I know a better way to achieve that," the statement is going to be in conflict with whatever the status quo is, and its proponents.

Avoiding conflict is an important aspect of Japanese society. As discussed previously it permeates the Japanese language in the way people speak. Avoidance of conflict also influences how people behave, particularly when the conflict is potentially with one's superiors in a company. In Japan, more than most places, I have found that managers and staff alike are deathly afraid of saying something that diverges from what the boss thinks, or perhaps more accurately, what they think the boss thinks—they may not think this at all! Such people often believe that by doing so, they will bring retribution down upon themselves for having the audacity to challenge the boss.

The irony is of course that every CEO I have ever met tells me how he wishes his people would come up with ideas, make suggestions, and warn of pitfalls—even if what is said is in conflict with what they think. The bane of every leader is the yes-man. Every leader I have met is never quite sure whether they are being told what their people think they want to hear, rather than what they need to know.

To many managers, disagreeing with the boss is viewed as a form of treason. However, not all disagreement with the boss is the same. There are in fact two types of disagreement—disagreement over goals and disagreement over means. The problem is that many managers fail to make the distinction between the two.

Disagreement over goals, particularly over strategic goals, is the kind of disagreement that will get a manager into trouble, because that really is a kind of treachery. Once the leadership has decided on a strategy to shift from low-cost commodity services to a high-value expert consultative service which has few competitors, for example, it would be treacherous if a manager said, "I don't like the strategy," or worse, said nothing and undermined the strategy.

That is entirely different from disagreement on means. For example, if a manager said to their boss, "To make the transition to expert services, I think we would get better results faster if we sent our people directly to end users of our services rather than waiting for alliance partners to invite us in." This kind of disagreement is not treachery, because the end goals are still the same—it is merely a suggestion of a way to better achieve the end goals.

However, many managers will hold back on disagreement over means in order to avoid confrontation and opposing the boss. Most managers, however, would appreciate staff bringing up such ideas for consideration, even if they still disagree in the end. At least good managers would!

There is a time to debate goals, and a time to debate means. A healthy debate about options for achieving goals is positive. As a leader, let your people know that that is OK and encourage your managers to speak up. Reward them for it, even when you disagree or decide not to take their advice. After all, isn't it the behavior of proactive thinking and advising you that you want, not necessarily that you always agree?

If you can set this example with senior leaders at your level, you can then encourage them to do the same with their staff, and so on down through the organization. However, the behavior must start at the top.

In Japanese, Japan or things Japanese are often referred to as *wa,* literally meaning harmony. Harmony is extremely important in the minds of Japanese people. In working with groups of senior leaders in companies, I often hear, "What we need around here is more *harmony.*" Yet, what is usually needed is not *more harmony*—people being more collegial with each other, more circumspect, and careful to avoid awkward confrontations—but rather *less* harmony, where issues can be aired without fear of personal repercussion.

The irony about harmony is that if you make harmony a goal and set about eliminating anything that is not harmonious, you end up creating disharmony—often on a catastrophic scale. For example, discouraging dissent for the sake of harmony rarely has beneficial results, whether in an organization or in an authoritarian society. However, encouraging *constructive disharmony,* while it may be somewhat chaotic and cause all sorts of confrontations, actually leads to harmony and better results, whether the disharmony of democracy, the disharmony of market economics, or the disharmony of a collective endeavor such as running a business. Disharmony is a release valve that removes pressure. It is a force that helps an organization continuously find its balance on a constantly shifting surface. Disharmony in an organization, as long as it is healthy disharmony over means rather than goals, is constructive.

Constructive disharmony is what makes organizations harmonious. It allows them to react rapidly to external change, and to operate and perform at higher levels.

You can find additional resources on the topics discussed in this chapter and more at *www.relansa.co.jp.*

Eliminating Performance Gaps

E very company CEO with whom I speak talks about some aspect of the performance of their people that they wish to change or improve. In Japan, more than elsewhere, attempts at changing people take on a Sisyphean quality. There is a tendency to ascribe failure to close performance gaps to the so-called "uniqueness" of Japanese culture. However, as discussed in previous chapters, this is a red herring when it comes to other issues and the same is true when it comes to improving performance. The reason for failure lies not in cultural difference. Rather, there are two reasons:

1. Prescribing an improper treatment to the cause
2. Attempting to treat staff performance gaps before that of their managers

Even after implementing many of my recommendations in previous chapters to eliminate refraction layers, performance gaps may stubbornly persist. Once again, the principle of refraction still applies, even though a performance gap may appear to be a capability deficit among lower-level staff. You must resolve performance gaps at a mid-level of management as a prerequisite to addressing performance gaps perceived at more junior staff levels. Otherwise, you risk spending lots of time, effort, and money for little or no improvement.

Whenever a company experiences a performance gap, there is often a knee-jerk reaction to order more training. Before you can even utter the words "personal development plan," someone in human resources is already requesting quotes from training providers. This approach however is totally nuts. My Jewish grandmother, bless her soul, was a great believer in the healing powers of orange juice. You caught a cold? Drink some orange juice. You just suffered a hernia? Have some orange juice. No matter what ailed you, her answer was orange juice, always orange juice, and lots more orange juice! Crazy, right? Well in many companies, training is to managers what orange juice used to be to my grandmother. Just as orange juice isn't going to help your hernia because orange juice doesn't address the underlying cause, training isn't going to improve performance when the cause is different to not knowing how to do something properly—and, even then, training often doesn't address that cause particularly well, something that I will discuss later on in the book.

Fortunately, performance gaps are not as complicated as hernias and other bodily ailments, or at least shouldn't be. In fact, there are only three causes for performance gaps:

1. Skill deficit: "I don't know how to ..."
2. Attitude problem: "I don't want to ..."
3. Roadblock: "Even if I wanted to, I can't ..."

Each cause requires a distinct treatment.

Identifying and Treating Cause

There is no more powerful word in any language than "why." The most common mistake I see managers make is jumping to conclusions based on observation alone, or not asking enough "why" questions. It may take asking "why" several times to peel back the layers of the onion and get to the cause, but get there we will.

For example, a client of mine had a problem in that sales teams were avoiding pharmaceutical customers. Pharmaceutical companies make great customers because reorders can continue for decades, and margins tend to be high. In talking with sales staff about the problem, they would say things like, "We just don't know how to sell to the pharmas. We're never successful with them. So, we just don't bother anymore."

What at first glance appears to be an "I don't how to ..." problem for the staff, actually turns out to be an "I don't want to ..." problem for sales managers when we ask them "why?"

ME	Why don't you approach pharmaceutical companies?
SALES MANAGER	It's too hard to sell to them.
ME	Why do you say that?
SALES MANAGER	Because none of what we have to sell has regulatory approval.
ME	Why is that?
SALES MANAGER	The customer hasn't applied for approval.
ME	Well your competitors sell to pharmaceutical companies. Don't they have the same problem?
SALES MANAGER	Yes.
ME	So why is it possible for them, but not possible for you?
SALES MANAGER	The sales cycles are long—years long, in fact—because approval requires clinical trials.

ME	Why is that a problem?
SALES MANAGER	Because I have quarterly quota requirements as part of my job. If I have my staff go after the pharmaceutical companies, I won't make quota.
ME	Pharmaceutical sales may take a long time, but once your product is approved, don't sales continue for years? Why isn't this valuable?
SALES MANAGER	Well, it will benefit my successor, but not me. I will have been fired by then for not making quota.

Cause identified. Clearly not a skill gap of the sales manager and, at this point, there is no indication of a skill gap among the sales staff. Nor is there any indication of a roadblock either. This is clearly an attitude problem of the manager that is the result of the company's performance evaluation system which penalizes a desired behavior—she could end up losing her job by going after the pharmas.

Providing additional sales training on how to sell to pharmaceutical companies to the sales manager and/or her team, which was actually what the company had intended to do, wasn't going to work, simply because skill gap was not the root cause of the problem. Even if skill gap were a problem for the sales staff, addressing the skill gap of the staff without addressing the attitude problem of the manager would be just as ineffective—a classic refraction layer. After the evaluation system was modified to reward managers for approaching the pharmas, and progressing products through the customers' processes of formulation and trials, behavior changed.

Steve's Three E's of Performance Gap Treatments: Education, Enlightenment, and Empowerment

Once identified, cause can be treated. The table below lays out treatment for each of the three causes of performance gap.

TABLE 7.1 Steve's three E's of performance gap treatments

Cause	Illustrative Statement	Treatment
Skill deficit	"I don't know how to ..."	Education
Attitude problem	"I don't want to ..."	Enlightenment
Roadblock	"Even if I wanted to, I can't ..."	Empowerment

Education addresses the "I don't know how to ..." skill deficit. It
answers the question of how to do the job, and consists primarily of process and technique—for example, educating people in
how to identify interest quickly in a sales call, or otherwise move
on to other prospects. If the sales people want to do this but
don't know how, simply increasing incentive pay without education isn't going to have much impact, and may in fact make things
worse, as failure to receive a bonus will be viewed as punishment.

Enlightenment addresses the "I don't want to ..." attitude problem.
It answers the question of "what is in it for me to do it differently
rather than the way I prefer?" Enlightenment focuses on an individual's motivation and underlying beliefs. In the example above,
the sales team leader believes there is no benefit in targeting pharmaceutical companies because, although highly profitable for the
business in the long term, it is not profitable for her individually—
time to contract takes years, whereas she is evaluated on the quarterly sales results of her team. Change the evaluation system and
you change the rationale for behavior. More training or education
on how to sell to pharmaceutical companies for her and her team
clearly wasn't going to work.

Empowerment addresses roadblocks—"Even if I wanted to I can't
...", answering the question of how what I do changes the world
for the better for a customer. Empowerment focuses on demarcat-
ing clear authority, provision of resources, and visibility through
to outcomes for customers. For example, a manager who gives
authority to frontline customer service staff to resolve customer
complaints using budget up to a fixed amount is removing roadblocks with empowerment.

Let's look at how these are applied specifically to mid-level managers.
Remember, resolving performance gaps at a middle management layer is
an absolute prerequisite to resolving any performance gaps in organizational layers below. You cannot work bottom-up and succeed.

Education: You Don't Train Leaders; You Coach Them

If your company is paying for courses in leadership, sales management,
strategy, or any type of training that requires a classroom-type setting for

mid-level leaders, you are wasting your company's money and squandering your managers' time. You don't train leaders. You coach them. Coaching is the most effective way to achieve rapid performance improvement in mid-level managers, and for many of their staff for that matter. Unlike training, goals, metrics of progress and success, regular feedback and accountabilities must be part of the coaching process. The key to coaching is that the learning is applied to the real business of the manager more or less in real time. So rather than "having to take time out for training," coaching is not time out. Coaching is *time in*, and a highly effective use of time because coaching progresses the manager's actual work as a learning tool while at the same time improving effectiveness on current business initiatives.

Too many companies, particularly Japanese companies, simply move managers up through the ranks with little support or preparation, and then suffer a dearth when it comes to a capable leadership bench for executive-level positions. This, despite a surplus of people with the right titles. "But we have great leadership training courses," I often hear. If you want to ensure sufficient leadership bench at all levels of the organization, particularly at the top, cultivate leaders proactively with coaching and start early. More on that in Chapter 9.

Note that in order to develop a manager's leadership capability, the manager must already be in a leadership position of some type, whether a first-time leader with a team of two people or the head of a major division. Courses on leadership theory for people who have yet to become leaders themselves may be interesting but are rarely effective. Leadership is learned through practice in the real world, not from a textbook or slide deck. You must be able to put learning into practice immediately, otherwise it is very unlikely that it will be utilized.

Just as in sports, a coach must be willing to push those being coached, and make them feel uncomfortable without hesitation or fear of repercussion. Coaches confront, challenge, and don't stand for compromised goals.

Beware that coaching is not a commodity service in the way training courses often are, and not all coaches are equal. The investment in the right coach for a key manager can result in significant top-line growth for the company. The return on investment can be massive. Many international companies have global contracts with providers of coaching services and policies to use them exclusively, but clearing-house coaches are best avoided. The reasoning is simple. Coaches who work through a clearing-house sacrifice two-thirds or more of their earning potential both in commissions to the clearing-house and the fees they could otherwise have charged, all to have a company do their marketing for them. Do you really expect someone who doesn't possess the business acumen to acquire their own clients themselves—and are happy to forgo that kind of income—will be the kind of coach to help one of your key managers achieve raging success? Human resource departments are constantly seeking efficiencies, simplicities, and homogenization at the expense of strategic imperative, particularly *your* strategic imperative. Make your own choices when it is your strategic outcomes that are at stake.

Also, don't forgo using internal coaches. By internal coach, I mean *leader*. Every manager who has staff is a coach—or should be one. Coaching is part of leadership. The managers at my most successful client companies coach their staff regularly and have a process of periodic informal performance reviews that are more frequent than the ones mandated by human resources—more effective too for that matter. In fact, these informal reviews have nothing to do with human resources at all, and are completely between manager and staff person. Mid-level managers and non-managers alike, who have good coaches for a boss, improve performance rapidly; and good coaching will often lead to dramatic outcomes.

One of my Japanese clients implemented this system for half of their sales managers. The results? Dramatic improvement in sales results for the managers who used the system, one of whom has since been promoted to sales director of a major division, and another who is now a candidate for the Osaka branch manager. Not only that, their staff generally are also far happier in their positions because they feel that they are growing as a result of the support, and have tangible and frequent touchpoints with their managers and, through them, with the most senior decision makers at the firm. Communication also flows in the other direction, with senior management and the leadership better informed of the issues facing their sales managers on the ground.

Being a follower under a good leader-coach imparts leadership skill. It also has the tendency to grow your leadership bench in an organic manner. One of the staff under the manager who was promoted to director, is now a manager himself, and continuing the leader-coach approach. This is how you can institutionalize leadership development in your organization as a natural process that is part of daily work. Human resources isn't even involved, and no one has had to sit in a seminar room for training! Because coaching, by nature, requires close interaction, it also becomes easier to better gauge personal characteristics and "fit." Just as not all coaches are the same, neither are all candidates with management experience and potential. Asking your leadership team to coach means that they will develop a stronger comprehension of the strengths and weaknesses of those who they are coaching. This is just the sort of information that you need in order to conduct effective succession planning—particularly if you could deploy this kind of system company-wide.

Enlightenment: What's in it for Me?

In Japanese companies, an attitude problem is by far the most common of performance gap causes. And this is particularly true of attitude problems among mid-level managers. It is a result of years of seniority-based promotion and lifetime employment, whether formalized in policy or simply a matter of practice. Rakuten Ichiba, CEO of Hiroshi Mikitani, has said that when workers are overprotected, company performance and competitiveness suffer. I have found this to be true everywhere I have done business—not just in Japan, but also in the US, France, Hong Kong, and Australia. Country culture has nothing to do with it, although some countries are more protective of labor than others—think of France as compared to China's Special Administrative Region, Hong Kong.

Historic practices or not, the root of attitude problems, whether in Japan or elsewhere, lies in company culture and individual beliefs. To understand what the culture of a company is, all that is necessary is to observe which behaviors are rewarded, which are penalized, and which are treated with indifference. A belief on the other hand is an understanding of the world that an individual holds to be true *a priori*. Rewards and penalties can be adjusted to change behavior, whereas a person's beliefs are harder to change. If you change rewards and penalties and can achieve a change in beliefs as a result, you can change behavior and close performance gaps.

Adjusting Company Culture

People behave in ways that move them toward some reward, away from some penalty, or both. Rewards and penalties can be a part of deliberate company policies and practices, be an inadvertent result of the same, or otherwise simply be a part of the social environment over which a business has little direct control. An example of the last is the pressure to conform and avoid being the proverbial "nail that sticks up" in Japan.

When performance gaps are related to company culture, they typically fall into two categories:

1. Insufficient reward or indifference toward doing the right thing
2. Insufficient penalty or indifference toward doing the wrong thing

Examples of these are all around us in our working environments (and outside of those of course!), and can include bonuses for hitting sales targets, praise for exceptional customer service, a bonus for achieving a high score on an annual engagement survey of staff (although this one always seems to have measurement and interpretation issues), firing for sexual harassment, and so on.

However, when most people think of incentives, the most common ones that come to mind are monetary rewards, and promotion—which is also frequently linked to money and perks. There are, however, more than just these two levels. There are four in fact. I call these the Four R's: Respect, Recognition, Remuneration, and Responsibility. If you want to change culture by changing what is rewarded and penalized, these are your levers. Pull them all.

The Levers of Motivation: The Four R's

Sieyu-Walmart's CEO Steve Dacus once said it best when asked, "What's the difference between motivating Japanese staff to change at Seiyu in Japan as opposed to American staff at Walmart in the United States?"

"Nothing." was his answer. "There is no difference between Japanese and Americans when it comes to what we value and what motivates us to change. Everyone wants to be treated with respect and recognized for a job well done. We need to stop thinking of people as being different because of where they come from. Fundamentally, we are all the same."

Like Steve Dacus, I have found this to be true everywhere I have done business—the US, Japan, Australia, France, Hong Kong, and elsewhere.

I don't care if someone is Japanese, American, French, Australian, Chinese, or North Korean. Human values are universal, and if you can tap into these, people will change for the better.

Respect

Everyone wants to be treated with dignity, no matter what they may happen to do for work or the person they happen to be. I talked with a staff person of Lenovo Japan's, and he told me this about the CEO Rod Lappin: "You know, I've had a lot of bosses, and when in their presence, I feel how important they are, particularly if they're the CEO. But when I'm with Rod, he makes me feel I'm important. He makes people feel good about themselves." This anecdote may feel like flattery, but it contains an important lesson. A true leader does not need to be sociable, but they do need to be able to personally recognize the critical importance of the people who are performing critical work for them. Some of you will recall the image of President Obama fist-bumping a cleaner in the White House. There is no doubt that the image was released for political spin, and in our age of doubt it is difficult to convince everyone that the moment could truly have been unscripted. However, putting aside the politics, simply focus on the image itself. There is no false jollity being displayed by the President, and it is not a moment of silliness or even celebration. What is being depicted is "respect"—acknowledgment that here is another human being who, although obviously not in the highest possible elected office, is still worthy of respect. It is also recognition for good work being done (more on that below) and in both senses it is an example to emulate.

Recognition

Recognition means more than most managers think. On surveys of leaders and the people they lead, recognition is always ranked high as a motivator by those being led—it often ranks higher than money, whereas leaders typically rank recognition lower than money. Don't underestimate the power of appreciation, which costs nothing most of the time.

A client of mine, the CEO at a service company in Japan, personally calls up frontline service people to say congratulations whenever a customer contacts the company to praise the service received. You can imagine the shock of the Japanese staff person receiving such a call from upon high. The Japanese may be outwardly unmoved, but inside they beam with pride when praised in such a way.

Jason Evans, the Kiwi CEO of Smith-Medical Japan, implemented an "Attaway" award for staff who perform well. Any manager or colleague can nominate someone for the award. Jason reviews each one personally. These awards are taken seriously in the company. Given that they are completely voluntary, their numbers also serve as an indicator of staff engagement and motivation.

Remuneration

Whenever there is talk of incentives, people always think money is the answer. It is in some cases, but that is rarer than people think, particularly at the mid-level management layer. Don't get me wrong. You need to compensate managers fairly for the job they do and people need to feel they are earning enough money to support the lifestyle they want or feel they deserve. However, once those ends are achieved, money tends to make little difference in motivating different behavior, and can even harm performance levels, particularly incentive-based pay schemes in mid-level management.

Over breakfast at the Tokyo American Club with the CEO of major fast-moving consumer goods company in Japan, I was asked my views on incentive-based pay systems, and whether or not I thought he should introduce one for a class of managers. I responded like this.

ME	Think of yourself, how you work, and your career. You're a diligent and ambitious guy. You always perform at your best because it's who you are. In fact, I suspect it would be difficult for you to perform less than your best deliberately. You wouldn't even know how, right?
CEO	Yes, this is true.
ME	So, let's take the job you're doing now. If I said I was going to pay you an additional $500,000 for top performance, is there is anything that you would actually change in the way you are doing things now without that additional monetary incentive?
CEO	No, I wouldn't. I'm already doing my best and doing what I believe is best for the business.
ME	You're saying the money wouldn't alter your behavior, right?

CEO	Right.
ME	So what makes you think that the top-performing managers in your organization are any different from you?
CEO	OK. I see your point. But what about the mediocre performers?
ME	What about them? Do you think that they perform the way they do because of the money?
CEO	No. I think it's something else.
ME	Do you think they will suddenly become ambitious, growth-oriented learners who like to take on a challenge, simply because you offer to pay them more?
CEO	Unlikely.
ME	OK. Now, let's talk about your top performers again. Don't you think they would be insulted if you suddenly introduced an incentive pay system?
CEO	Are you kidding? I think they would love it.
ME	But aren't you really telling them that you don't trust them to continue doing a good job for you—that now you need this carrot and stick to motivate them like beasts of burden, as opposed to the values-driven competent respected professionals they are? After all, they were achieving results without the monetary incentive before.
CEO	I hadn't looked at it that way.
ME	Might they not begin to think that things have changed in your company for the worse—you don't value people in the same way anymore and you don't value them. It's all a financial transaction now. And because they are top performers, they probably don't worry about finding another job should they choose to quit. Top people are always confident that they can find work. It's the mediocre people who will stick with you forever out of fear they won't ever find another well-paying job.
CEO	So what are you saying?
ME	Implementing a pay for performance system may actually reduce performance overall in your company. Your

top performers at best will simply continue working the way they do now and at worst will become disillusioned and leave. Your mediocre performers will not likely be moved to do any better than they are doing now.

CEO   OK. I need to rethink this.

Pay your managers fairly, but avoid monetary incentives as a way to improve performance. Treat your best managers well, and this means market rate or, in exceptional circumstances, above it; and do what you can to support personal growth—such as coaching—but cull the mediocre once attempts at support have played out. Offering more money to the mediocre certainly won't change them or the way in which they perform for you.

Responsibility

You motivate managers by challenging them. Increase their responsibility. People are not motivated by what is easy, they are driven by what is hard. A senior executive coaching client of mine, when asked what he wanted to achieve as a result of our work together, told me among other things, "I am responsible for Japan right now, but I want to be responsible for China and Korea as well. I can handle all of North Asia, and I want to."

Intrigued, I asked why? Was it for more money, more prestige, more perks? No, none of these things. In fact, he did not expect a pay rise as a result.

"Look, I've been in Japan doing this kind of work for years now. I'm already good at it and it is easy for me, but there is no further personal growth. I'm bored. I like learning, and this is the next challenge."

Steve's Three Physical Laws of Motivation

So the Four R's of motivation—Respect, Recognition, Remuneration, and Responsibility—are the levers of motivation, and you can change culture by shifting these. However, it's not as simple as that. You still have to contend with *Steve's Three Physical Laws of Motivation*.

Law #1: Every well-intended incentive spawns an equal and opposite incentive with unintended results.

To illustrate this, an example might be a service company that performs maintenance, repair, and regulatory inspections of building equipment. The company rewards managers for productivity—the meeting of a quota of inspections and their timely completion, meeting sales and profitability targets, and net gains in the building of contract numbers. That's great for sales, profits, productivity, and happy customers, as fast inspections reduce inconvenient equipment downtime during inspection, but it has also spawned some sinister behavior. Inspectors perform cursory checks on some checklist items to save time. They frequently give a pass on grey area irregularities which might otherwise require additional time to resolve, in order to avoid reducing productivity levels. Despite a company values statement of "safety first" hanging framed in writing in every office and meeting room of the company worldwide, safety has been compromised by the incentives. And, unfortunately, accidents have also occurred.

Management, alarmed by this, sought the cause and determined that the inspectors still lacked technical skill in identifying irregularities, and worked too slowly to maintain quality and productivity targets. A series of training workshops was ordered company-wide. Despite this, random spot-checks of inspectors' work revealed a continuing high rate of irregularities, some of which were serious safety risks.

It had never occurred to the executive leadership team that the reward for business results targeted primarily at the managers could be the cause of the undesired behavior. In fact, when I first brought it up, the team was incredulous. However, the evidence from interviews, asking multiple layers of "why?" questions, was hard to ignore.

Why don't managers see these unintended results? Simply because they tend to focus on the intended results of an incentive to the extent that they are blindsided by the unintended ones and the unforeseen behaviors they spawn. To avoid this, we must examine each incentive, policy, and practice and imagine possible side-effects. Talk with people about their views, particularly if it is their behavior you hope to change. For existing performance gaps, talk with people about the reasons for their behavior. Look for patterns of rationale to map out the actual drivers of behavior, not just the intended ones. It is possible to change behaviors by adjusting the incentives, but as you do, be aware of other possible unintended consequences. Involve other people from the organization in the discussion as you make changes, and perhaps even speak to some trusted outsiders. You need a varied range of perspectives, including some neutral ones, to get this right.

For example, in the inspection case above, one possible adjustment might be including irregularity identification as part of productivity, so it is not so much an exception that throws off the flow of work, but rather a part of the job that is rewarded when handled. A possible side-effect may be oversensitivity to irregularities and an overwhelming number of exceptions, so the company might decide that irregularities should be handled by a separate team specialized in first validating them. The key is to think beyond the obvious and immediate.

Law #2: A reward now is better than a better reward later, even if it precludes the latter. Corollary: Avoiding a penalty now is better than a reward later, even if the former may ultimately result in a greater penalty.
This is one of the reasons it can be so difficult to get managers to improve English ability when they have no immediate need for the language, or if even the thought of opening an English text elicits traumatic memories from their youth. Law #2 also, in part, explains the previous example of the safety inspectors, because avoiding the penalty for lower productivity is immediate, whereas an accident, which is almost guaranteed should a number of inspections prove to be substandard, may be way off in the distant future.

The way individuals counter Law #2 is with discipline. I know if I exercise hard now rather than eating that cheesecake, I will have a nice body in the future, but man is it hard to do that! Not everyone has the same capability for discipline, and company goals may not carry the same weight as individual ones. So, we need to sweeten the pot by providing some kind of immediate reward that will tide a manager over to the reward in the future. The way to do this is to reward behaviors and not just results.

So, for example, in motivating managers to learn English, rather than giving them yearly TOEIC score targets, which in themselves have questionable correlation with English ability anyway, reward the behaviors needed to learn a language regardless of level or result. A point system with options is one way. Award points for things like attending conversation classes, giving an internal presentation in English, giving an external presentation in English, publishing an article in English in a trade journal, holding a business meeting with a customer in English, and so on. Require achieving so many points per month, quarter, etc. This is a way of throwing some tangible support behind a person's own natural aptitude for self-discipline. No matter how people choose to go about earning the points, English capability will improve, because people will be behaving like language learners. The results will come later.

Law #3: Beliefs trump incentives.

For example, the top internal candidate for the CEO role at an international financial institution in Japan believes that non-Japanese managers are incapable of working with their Japanese teams. He refuses to consider non-Japanese for any C-level position. Apart from the ethical, legal, and corporate values implications, such a practice may severely hamper competitive capability, the ability to attract and retain top talent at all levels, and long-term financial performance.

Yet, it is unlikely that incentives, either positive or negative, will cause this manager to abandon his belief. Incentives may achieve compliant behavior in this case, as opposed to real commitment to company values. For example, the new CEO decides to put a foreigner in a C-level position for the purpose of compliance, but establishes a shadow position with a Japanese manager who has the real power, authority, budget, and a staff.

The only thing you can do to deal with Law #3 is try to reason with the manager about the belief in the hope of changing it. Ask for the rationale. Ask for evidence supporting the belief. Provide examples of where the belief does not hold true; for example, "So, do you really mean to tell me that Carlos Ghosn, CEO of Nissan, isn't capable of managing his Japanese team?!"

Beliefs are among the hardest things to change in people's thinking. If you don't believe me, try changing someone else's view on God or the merits of their preferred political party. In fact, it is unlikely you will be able to change the key beliefs of another person, and even if you thought you had, you may never know because you cannot peer into another person's mind. All you can do is observe behavior as an indicator. If you cannot achieve the change in behavior, and you suspect it is a belief-related as opposed to incentive-related issue, you have a choice—live with it, or remove the manager—but make the decision and don't dally. There is nothing more costly to a business than a key manager with unchangeable, counterproductive behavior.

Empowerment: What I Do Makes the World Better for a Customer, and I Can See the Outcome

Empowerment is not equivalent to bestowing authority, although clear authority and the will to use it is part of empowerment. The key to empowerment is a belief that a person can change the world for the better. In the corporate context, this can be refined to changing the world for the better for a customer through their own work. The customer can be an internal or external one, or a combination of both. That requires three things (Figure 7.1):

1. The authority to act and the will to use it
2. The resources to achieve the desired outcome
3. Visibility of the outcome for the customer

If any one of these is missing, the result is an "enweakenment" mentality, and the roadblocks it spawns:

1. Self-centered mentality: "That's someone else's job."
2. Poverty mentality: "I know, but we just don't have the [time/money/people] to do that."
3. Helplessness mentality: "Don't ask me—I just work here!" or in Japan, "Our policy is ..."

If individuals have authority to act and the will to use it and the resources are available to achieve desired outcomes, but visibility through to customer outcomes is limited, then what you have is a self-centered mentality. This is common among managers of back office departments far

FIGURE 7.1 Empowerment's three essentials

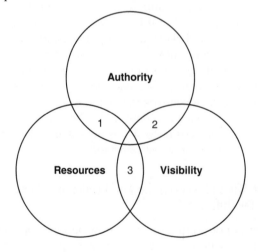

removed from the customer. Attitude is exemplified by expressions like, "That's not our job," or "That's the sales division's problem."

If there is visibility of customer outcomes and authority, plus the will to use it but a lack of resources, that spawns a poverty mentality. Managers feel they must have staff make up for the poverty with elbow grease. Particularly in Japan—where selfless, stoic perseverance in righteous yet hopeless causes is seen as a virtue—poverty mentality may cause your managers to risk their health and well-being, all to protect the business of the firm. Managers will intervene frequently with inefficient and often ineffective heroic acts of rescue, and attempt to cheerlead a gung-ho attitude among staff as much as they can to keep people from giving up, assuming they have not given up themselves. Poverty mentality is exemplified by expressions like, "We just don't have the [resource] to do that!" or "We'll just have to make do!" or "What's the work-around?"

If there is visibility and resources, but a lack of authority or a lack of will to use it, that spawns a helplessness mentality. Managers feel as if they are awash in a tumultuous sea, with no choice but to go where winds blow them and the waves throw them. Helplessness mentality is exemplified by expressions like, "Don't ask me, I just work here," or what may be more common in Japan, "Company policy is ..."

The thing about roadblocks is that they always ultimately limit value to the customer. For example, the Japan office of an American equipment manufacturer in Japan has a global marketing division in its head office that dictates quotas of products to sell in foreign markets. Some of the products aren't well suited to Japan's market needs, whereas others are. Sales people know they could achieve better results if they could choose which products to offer their customers, but they lack the authority to do so. In the end, it is the customer who suffers, perhaps without even knowing it, because the sales people are not able to offer products that may well have been valuable to them.

In a different Japanese company that manufactures and sells chemical ingredients, the administration department that handles factory orders is so obsessed with the smooth running of its department that it refuses to process certain orders that it probably could, given adequate notice and planning. Yet, there is little motivation to undertake such planning. While sales people are frustrated because they are losing orders to competitors, people in the administration department see nothing but smooth sailing because their department is hitting key efficiency targets. They consider managing customer complaints the realm of the sales people, and separate from their work. "Why can't the sales people just explain to the customer what our needs are?", they ask in all seriousness. They have no visibility through to customer outcomes, or perhaps they simply choose not to look.

In yet another company, a fulfillment division is plagued with service problems—lost inventory, late deliveries, billing mistakes, etc. Staff work long hours during harried days, resolving exceptions and putting out fires, all because there is no budget made available to integrate disparate IT systems that had been cobbled together from businesses of various acquired companies. They view the company as poor (even though it isn't). Staff turnover is high and, as a result, customer service is poor and the stream of complaints constant.

Empowering Empowerment

Removal of roadblocks may require intervention of a leader, but it does not necessarily have to if you establish a framework for managers and staff to use independently. Some of the most common roadblocks in companies in Japan and elsewhere in the world involve how two departments work with each other—usually a customer-facing one and a support one, such as sales and R&D, sales and marketing, customer service and sales, IT and everybody else.

At one of my Japanese clients, Nikko Chemicals, I helped establish what we decided to call a "Cross-Functional Forum." The concept is simple. Two collaborating departments with points of contention come together on neutral ground to resolve them. They each present the goals they need to achieve, and how each depends on the other to help them achieve those goals. Rather than blaming each other for problems, the rule is to simply explain the impact of the work of the other department on the work of the one presenting, both positive and negative. The outcome for the customer always remains at the center of the discussion. Both department teams then work together to come up with a better way to achieve a better outcome for the customer, as opposed to a fixation on their work in the context of the specific department.

When both sides reach agreement, they each make commitments to the other on how they will change the way they work together. Those commitments are published on the company's intranet, for everyone to see. Every manager has the right to request a forum session with another. Countless roadblocks have been resolved in the business without requiring the intervention of a senior leader. The practice continues to this day.

Performance Improvement Decision Tree

The decision tree below is meant to help you decide an effective approach to performance, presenting the options discussed in this chapter.

FIGURE 7.2 Closing performance gaps

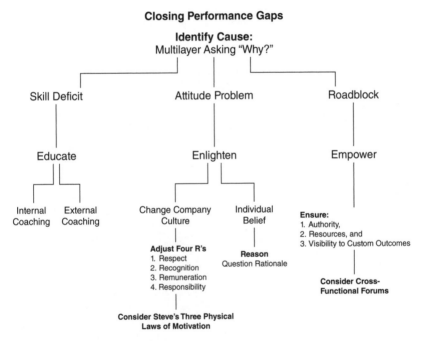

Law #1: Every well-intended incentive spawns an equal and opposite incentive with unintended results.

Law #2: A reward now is better than a better reward later, even if it precludes the latter. **Corollary:** Avoiding a penalty now is better than a reward later, even if the former may ultimately result in a greater penalty.

Law #3: Beliefs trump incentives.

To be clear, in treating performance gaps you must address higher-level layers of management before you can address lower-level layers of management and/or staff. Doing otherwise will result in your efforts being deflected by the refraction layer. The treatment for any performance gap is contingent upon the three possible causes: skill deficit, attitude problem, and roadblock. Choose the appropriate treatment, and you will get results.

You can find additional resources on the topics discussed in this chapter and more at *www.relansa.co.jp*.

CHAPTER 8

They Got It Wrong! It's NOT a Marathon, but Lots of Sprints!

O nce refraction layers have been more or less eliminated in an organization's layers of mid-level management, an organization is capable of moving with remarkable speed and agility. So many processes used in companies for business change and improvement—such as strategy development, business cases for investment in capability changes, innovation, and individual growth and development—are more convoluted than they need to be and performed less frequently than they ought to be. In this chapter, I discuss how you can achieve lightning-like speed in all of these, once refraction is under control.

If you are a distance runner, and you want to achieve rapid improvement in performance, you don't do so by running a lot of long distances—you do so by performing lots of little sprints. Whether preparing for a marathon, or simply wanting to be able to run longer and/or faster, sprinting is the way to go. This works not just for running, but also for cycling, swimming, and likely a number of other endurance sports. Athletes call it *interval training,* and it is proven to get better results and faster at that.

For many people who take fitness seriously, this is counterintuitive. Whether in New York's Central Park or around the Imperial Palace moat in Tokyo, you will find lots of runners intent on pushing themselves as hard as they can, huffing and puffing as they make their way, all in the name of fitness or perhaps also in order to lose weight.

For some reason, this kind of chronic cardio activity has become the ideal of fitness for many. I have done cardio like this too, thinking it was beneficial to lose weight and get fit, only to discover later that often the opposite is true. Chronic cardio sends a signal to the brain to increase fat storage. After all, to the brain it looks like you're going to need the fat later given all the cardio activity you are doing now. Chronic cardio also signals the body to consume muscle tissue for energy, weakening you as your body consumes itself! If you have ever seen an avid runner with a wraith-like body, this is what has happened in the extreme. The brain reasons that the body needs the fuel now, and the extra bulk of muscle only slows it down. Our brains are not stupid. Why would I possibly want to do a fitness activity that can cause me to retain fat and lose muscle? The reality is that many people do just that, simply because they don't realize the effect.

In many companies, managers approach business like training through long-distance running. For example, many managers and staff are forced endure long workshops to develop strategy. Then, like preparing for a long-distance race, they plan to execute a strategy for at least a year, at the end of which time victory or defeat will be determined.

"Long-distance running" in business can have a similar impact on the organization to the one it can have on the human body. I have witnessed this approach to strategy consume the "muscle" of a business, as managers spend a disproportionate amount of time measuring, analyzing, and justifying results as opposed to achieving them. There are endless meetings and reviews. Staff are forced to gather data for reporting on arcane KPIs. In the same way that chronic cardio signals the body to store fat, a chronic cardio approach to strategy encourages some managers to deliberately set targets they know they can exceed with ease. Others mask achievements early in the year so they show a burst of achievement later on, like conserving energy for a decisive sprint at the finish line. Like our brains, middle managers are not stupid. They know the score.

And then there is the trance-like state of the distance runner. Like marathoners who become numb to the world around them and their own discomfort, turning their bodies into running automatons, I have watched managers go through the motion of performing on a strategy set months previously, numb to new developments in the business environment or to the havoc wreaked internally in the organization, determined to push on through. Ignoring the pain around them, they stay the course, and endure until the finish of the cycle. Others simply abandon strategy altogether. Too hard. Too painful. Just like the runner who has given up on running.

Sprinting in business improves performance rapidly in the same way that it does in endurance sports. Frequent short bursts of sustained energy are more effective than long sustained efforts. Business can be used for strategy, innovation, business cases, and personal growth. As a leader you can achieve rapid improvement by sprinting with staff, and each of your managers should make sprinting part of their routine, just as a proficient coach uses sprinting with their athletes.

The Strategy Sprint

Strategy is always developed by describing a future state and working backwards. While this may seem obvious, in my experience an inordinate amount of time in strategy development is spent by senior and middle-level managers on analyzing the past, or otherwise developing a strategy that merely assembles current capabilities to hit relatively straightforward strategic goals, without much change in how business is conducted, or what might be achieved other than simply the same as last year except more of it. Strategy development exercises frequently turn into future prediction exercises. By that I mean the managers participating hedge their risk by proposing strategy based on doing what they know they already can do, and achieving what they know they already can achieve (or in some cases have already achieved), all within a comfortable timeframe. The strategy development exercise becomes one of avoiding commitment to achieving difficult goals to which one will be held to account, and assuring one's own position in the organization. Strategy then becomes a push—pull tug-o-war between managers who wish to protect themselves and leaders who need to move the organization forward and demonstrate results to a board and/or superiors in headquarters. The exercises tend to be long and painful at times, replete with full-on, hours-long presentations accompanied by slides with complicated charts and numbers, all meant to justify the correctness of the choice of path. I have never met a middle-level manager who is energized by this kind of approach to strategy. Not only is this approach ineffective, it takes an enormous amount of time. Strategy development does not have to be this way.

In every organization with which I have worked on strategy, I have been able not only to help shorten strategy development time, but also help develop a bolder strategy that achieves results upon execution. Below are nine ways to accelerate strategy development.

Convene Shorter Sessions More Frequently as Opposed to Longer Sessions Infrequently, Such as Annually

There is nothing sacrosanct about the annual strategy review or three-year plan. More frequent and rapid strategy reviews and development keep strategic objectives in the forefront of managers' minds, and allow for more rapid adjustment to seize business opportunities, address changes in the business environment, and revisit assumptions upon which the strategy was based. It encourages managers to think critically frequently, as opposed to being lulled into the comfort of a routine. Consider strategy sprints quarterly or at least once every six months. Feel free to call for a strategy sprint whenever you think it might be beneficial or necessary, in the same way parliamentary governments call for elections. For example, you may decide a strategy sprint must be held no longer than six months after the previous one in principle, but be open to mandating one whenever you think it is appropriate, such as when there is a significant development in the market that had not been foreseen. You don't necessarily need to follow a schedule.

Stop Analyzing the Past

Overanalysis of past performance tends to lead to more of doing more of the same thing, perhaps just a little bit better. It effectively leads more frequently to *shminnovation* rather than innovation. It limits thinking about goals to those that are considered to be reasonable purely based on what has been achieved in the past as opposed to bold objectives based on what has not yet been tried. Rather than querying the past, a better question to start with might be, "Who are our future customers, and will they buy from us? Are they the same as our current customers, or different?"

Stop Analyzing Your Perceived Competition

The more time spent on analyzing competition, the more one's company begins to look like the competition. Strategy will tend to become reactive to competitors' moves, as opposed to disruptive toward competitors. Overanalysis of competitors can also be limiting, as it allows the competition to define your business model, often without your being conscious of it. For example, in working with an expert services company in the business of testing chemical formulations for consumer products, the CEO said, "We're a small company with limited staff. If we want to grow our revenues, we can only do so by scaling up. We would need to have staff numbers like our competitors if we wanted to increase market share."

ME	So what you're saying is that to grow your business, you can only do so by doing more of what you currently do, for which you would need more staff like your competitors. Right?
CEO	Exactly.
ME	Why do you have to imitate the model of your competitors?

CEO   That is simply the way companies work in this industry.

ME   Well, why can't you grow your business by increasing the value of the services you provide with the same staff? The difference between you and your competitors is not just staff numbers. Your staff are all highly expert in their fields, and are able to advise clients in a way that your competitors can't. Your competitors rely more on quantity of standard testing products and methods because they don't have your expertise.

CEO   Go on.

ME   You told me that your highest margin services are the ones that are the most consultative, that require a high degree of expertise. Why not expand those, and drop the more commodity-like products and services?

The CEO did just that. The strategy resulted in a jump in sales and profitability without an increase in staff numbers.

Stop Debating the *How* When the *What* Is Not Clear or Agreed Upon

In strategy development discussions, I have found that an inordinate amount of time is wasted debating best possible actions—the *how*—when the desired outcomes—the *what*—is still unclear. For example, debating heatedly whether or not the company should cut out distributors is pointless without clearly identifying *what* you wish to achieve as a business outcome. If you say that you want to have an intimate relationship with customers so that you can address their needs better with your products, you have articulated the *what*. Cutting distributor relationships and going direct is now just one option among many, about which you can have a rational discussion of the merits and risks. Whether you are leading a strategy development session, facilitating one, or simply participating in one, cut the debate on means when ends are still unclear and you can accelerate the process.

Create the Future as Opposed to Attempting to Divine the Future

Many managers become tentative when developing strategy because they believe they are being asked to divine the future. For example, when

I have facilitated strategy development sessions and asked a manager, "How much in sales do you want to target for the Indonesian market?", I frequently get a response like, "I don't know. I don't have enough data. I can't say how much we will sell."

Yet that was not my question. In strategy, you never quite know with certainty what you will achieve. The point is to articulate what you *want* to achieve, and then work backwards from that.

The hemming and hawing over goals and targets not only wastes time—as managers sit silently with furled brows as if the sheer brute force of brain power will produce the answer they want. Progress is slowed.

You have to put a stop to that. I usually say something like, "Forget about what you think is possible now and don't worry if you have no idea what is possible. If you could, what would you *want* to achieve? Don't worry about the how now. We'll deal with that later."

Focus on What Can Go Wrong and How to Deal with Contingency as Opposed to Justifying the Right Path

In my experience coaching senior leaders who are preparing for strategy development sessions, including CEOs preparing for global strategy development sessions at their headquarters, there is a lot of time spent on preparing data to justify a course of action. And I mean *lots* of data. I have seen presentations that include more than one hundred slides' worth of data.

Most of this is pointless, first because no one can absorb such a quantity of data and interpret it in any meaningful way, particularly if this is one presentation of many; and second, because if just one of the assumptions turns out to be wrong, the course of action could be completely invalidated. For example, a client company had plans to roll out a premium product manufactured in Southeast Asia with the same quality as the Japanese-produced equivalent but at a slightly lower price (but a much higher price than the non-premium competition). Success of the product was predicated on a key assumption: customers care enough about the higher grade to pay more for it now and would continue to do so in the future. That assumption turned out to be incorrect. Customers were happy with the lower grade alternative, as the higher quality product made no difference to their business.

In my experience, such presentations, while rich in data, rarely contain explicit assumptions, but rather implicit ones. A far more effective presentation would be a shorter one that presents a recommended course of action with assumptions upon which it is based. An assumption is always the mirror image of a risk in that you need to ask the following:

1. What if the assumption turns out to be wrong?
2. When will we know whether or not the assumption is valid? How can we find out sooner?
3. What is the contingency should the assumption be wrong?

Rather than long justifications of actions, a sober list of assumptions, when and how they will be validated, and what the contingencies are should the assumptions turn out to be wrong, is not only faster to present but also a more robust recommendation, because it allows for being wrong or for situations to change. This is also a move away from trying to divine the future and toward creating the future you want for the business.

Follow the 10-20-30 Rule of Slide Presentations

If slide presentations are absolutely necessary, insist that they are concise, easy to understand, and readable from the back of the room:

- 10 slides
- 20 minutes
- 30-point font

Longer presentations are difficult to follow anyway, and little is retained from them, and no one can read anything smaller than 30-point font unless they happen to be in their twenties, a trained United States Marine sniper, and sitting in the front row. These guidelines keep presentations useful and short.

Detail can be saved for questions and discussion. So, if a manager insists on having an 80-slide deck, fine. However, he doesn't present slides unless germane to a question or discussion.

So if a manager is allotted say an hour for a presentation, they will present for 20 minutes. Then there are 40 minutes available for questions and discussion. Many mid-level managers attempt to convince other managers and superiors that they know what they are talking about by presenting lots of data in slides. In a two-hour presentation, there may be 10 or 15 minutes of questions and discussion—if people are still awake! Managers should report only what others need to know, not everything that they themselves know.

Nothing is more persuasive than pithiness and brevity. Nothing convinces others that you know what you are talking about more than to be able to respond to questions, rather than reading from slides. The best presentations are the ones that are brief and engaging, and that should be the ideal. Not only is it more effective, it's fast! Your audience will be awake and engaged, and if you happen to be able to wrap up before the end of your allotted time, they will love you!

Stop Giving Background; State Conclusions First

Many managers, when explaining something, tend to explain background as a narrative preceding a climactic conclusion. I have found that this not only takes time, background often does not aid in understanding. As a rule, insist on stating conclusions first and allow others to ask for background if needed.

The same goes for questions. When a manager wants to ask a question, insist that they ask the question first rather than narrating a long background to set up the question. Allow others to ask for background when they feel they need it. Most of the time, they won't!

Encourage ownership of strategy, not ownership of the business

In some companies, strategy is made by the leader behind closed doors and then rolled out. In most companies, however, it is a collective exercise. Involving more people in the organization leads to better alignment —people moving toward the same goals, and a greater sense of ownership. People are far more likely to support a strategy that they had a hand in crafting as opposed to a strategy that was imposed upon them.

I am in favor of anything that helps with an increased sense of ownership among managers and staff. However, taking ownership of strategy is not the same as taking ownership of the business. Salaried managers cannot take the business in a direction simply because it is what they desire.

For example, the CEO of the Japan subsidiary of a European client company of mine was preparing to involve the senior leadership in strategy development. He stated in clear terms that the company is in the business of its core agrotech product. How best to take the business forward was an objective of the strategy development. However, being in the business of that product was not up for debate, though some managers wished to debate it. In the end, this was a decision for the owners who have a financial stake of the business, not a decision for the employees.

I have found that some leaders wish to encourage debate on subjects, even though they have already decided what the decision needs to be, only to give a sense of ownership to the managers. Not only does this kind of futile debate waste time, it results in frustrating employees as they sense they have been making arguments for something that has already been decided for them. It makes them feel patronized, which never helps in giving a sense of ownership. Be clear about the boundaries upfront. While some may be disappointed if limited to an area they wish to debate, this is far better than the alternative of encouraging a debate for show, or worse—compromising strategy for the interests of those who have a job but no capital tied up in the business.

These are just a few ways to accelerate strategy development. There are others I have not listed here. In fact, you can probably come up with some on your own. It isn't necessary to adopt all of these, but for your next strategy development activity, consider adopting some. See what the result is and decide what works best for you and your team.

Innovation Sprint

I was talking with the general manager of a well-known hospitality organization in Japan about innovation. The business is very successful, and comes up with a lot of excellent ideas that are put into practice. However, the business is facing a new period of expansion in which it will need a greater number of innovative ideas that will grow parts of the services business in order to achieve the new and ambitious financial targets.

ME   Where do new ideas come from?

GM   We have a revenues team that uses business intelligence analytics to mine for opportunities. Executives sometimes approach me with ideas. Sometimes, we are approached by external businesses that suggest partnerships of some type. There is also an employee suggestion box that gets used. However, most of those ideas have to do with improving the workplace and don't specifically address ideas for business growth.

ME   Do you do any kind of guided ideation activities with general staff?

GM   No. We have never done anything like that.

Don't get me wrong. This is a highly innovative organization, one of the best I have encountered. However, failing to take advantage of staff for ideation in a proactive way is like a farmer who leaves fertile fields fallow and cultivates only what happens to grow on them. Serendipity is not an innovation strategy.

In the previous chapter, I discussed ideation as the starting point of any innovation process. You can accelerate innovation by holding an ideation sprint. It is not that difficult, and does not require using large of amounts of time or tie up valuable resources.

As of the time of writing this chapter, I have just led one with a client company that had never done any kind of organized ideation before. The CEO had been lamenting that new product development was slowing, and the products that were coming out had only marginal impact— *shminnovation* as opposed to innovation.

We held a half-day ideation session that resulted in no less than 40 new product ideas, five of which were given priority for next step in the company's product development process. One idea has the potential of generating tens of millions of dollars in additional profits for the company, and as development progresses along with discussions with customers, it looks like the idea will go to market. That idea came from a junior-level salesperson. Now this was the result of a half-day workshop with a group that had never done ideation in an organized way.

What would happen if this same group repeated this exercise every two months? What if they took a full day or two days to cover more themes? Imagine the results.

Not all ideas will make it. Most ideas, even good ideas, simply won't work, and there is nothing wrong with that. Ideation is a game of quantity more than quality. I have helped companies go from ten product ideas per year to 300, increasing products brought to market tenfold. The investment in time is minimal, and the results can come very fast.

Recall from the last chapter, that ideation isn't just about new products, but new processes, new technologies, new market segments in new industries, and new ways of selling to customers. You can hold an innovation sprint session on any of these themes.

Business Case Sprint

Many mid-level managers with whom I have worked have talked about how they have requested budget for a resource of some type but are either denied or simply get no response from their managers. Projects and plans then languish, or productivity suffers. When I ask whether or not the manager made a business case, the response frequently is no, and sometimes, "What's a business case?"

For example, a director of a small sales team complained that his sales people spend nearly half the day simply doing routine paperwork related to orders rather than going out and selling.

ME	Could this routine paperwork be done by an administrative person?
DIRECTOR	Yes. We've hired people in the past for that, but in this team we have no one on staff.
ME	Why not hire one?
DIRECTOR	There is a hiring freeze in our company to reduce cost.
ME	Have you presented a business case?
DIRECTOR	No. I've only made the request. How would I make a business case?

Requests for resources without a business case merely sound like a cost increase to those with profit and loss responsibility. The business case is the response when asked, "Show me the money!" Every expenditure must be described in terms of an investment opportunity for the business. If a manager can show the payback in financial terms, the chances of approval increase tremendously, as does the speed of decision making.

If the money is not persuasive, and there is no other rational reason for denial, you are probably not talking with the right person—that is to say someone who has the authority to authorize an investment independently and who has fiduciary responsibility for the result, that is to say the economic owner of the problem. If you are not talking with the economic owner, you are wasting your breath, no matter how compelling the business case!

I advise managers to keep business cases simple. They have seven parts:

1. A description of the problem to resolve
2. The business outcome desired
3. Options for addressing the problem, which should always include the "Do nothing" option
4. Risks for each option
5. Monetary investment for each option
6. The expected payback on the bottom line, and the payback timeframe
7. The manager's recommended option and why

I recommend doing this in writing so they can be shared easily. It should take no more than a page. With an artifact like this, it is now possible to have a rational business discussion about the merits of the investment.

In the sales director example above, making the case for hiring the administrative assistant is pretty straightforward:

- Problem: Sales are spending nearly half their time on routine paperwork as opposed to being out selling for the business.
- Desired outcome: Maximize sales.
- Options:

1. Hire an additional sales person.
    a. Cost would be an additional $100,000 per year.
    b. Revenues would increase by about $2 million annually, adding $800,000 to the bottom line.

    c. Risks: Sales person could take up to two years to ramp up to full potential, or might not work out at all.

    d. Ultimately 8 to 1 return on investment.

1. Hire an administrative staff person.
   a. Cost would be about $40,000 per year.
   b. Revenues would increase by at least $800,000 per sales person for a team of five, total of $4 million, adding $1.6 million to the bottom line.
   c. Risks: Ramping up the admin person could take up to six months. New-hire might not work out, and quit or otherwise have to be terminated.
   d. Ultimately, an expected return of 40 to 1.

2. Continue as is.
   a. Outgoing cost is nil.
   b. I believe we are losing at least $2.4 million in revenue opportunity annually.
   c. Risks: Not only are we forgoing business, we are demoralizing sales people with non-sales work, and potentially losing customers to competitors in the long term.

I recommend Option 2, hiring an administrative staff person. Return on investment is extremely high at 40 to 1, at least five times greater than hiring additional sales staff, and time to ramp up is relatively short. I expect to add at least $2.4 million to the bottom line.

Simple and straightforward, isn't it? Well, not for all mid-level managers. When I describe this method, many balk at having to put the benefit of each option in *monetary* terms. Typically, there are three obstacles to this.

1. **Fear of committing themselves to a number, to which the manager will be held accountable.** For example, a manager with a superb idea for investment in a manufacturing capability—one that had clear and convincing return—told me, "I know the business case is great. But as soon as I suggest this, if it is approved, I will be made responsible for achieving the financial results, beyond what I have already committed to! If I don't get the results, my career is at risk! Why should I put myself at unnecessary risk?"

2. **Fear of not getting the amount of money right.** For example, a manager was looking for budget to help improve the leadership

capability of the team of managers below him, but when I asked, "If you were successful, how would that impact the bottom line?", he would not even venture a guess. If you won't express the benefit in financial terms, it is hard to make a convincing case for investment expenditure. Precise accuracy is rarely necessary, just order of magnitude. For example, are we talking thousands, tens of thousands, hundreds of thousands, or millions of dollars?

3. **Viewing any expenditure as a potentially avoidable cost as opposed to evaluating all expenditure as an investment opportunity for the business that improves financial performance.** Human resource departments are notorious for this in imposing blanket spending limits on coaching rates, training rates, and so on. For example, one manager complained to me that there was a global policy on coaching rates. Within the rate limit, he could hire coaches for his team in Japan, but none of them were capable of helping his team achieve the improvement in financial performance he was seeking. The few coaches he felt could do so were all out of his price range, even though there was ample return to justify the expenditure based on a conservative estimate of reasonable results.

As a leader, you can take action to help eliminate this kind of tentativeness. Below are some suggestions.

1. Educate managers in how to develop a business case.
2. Make a business case the standard way to request resources, and encourage managers to use it, not in a bureaucratic way for a finance department to sign off on, but rather as an artifact to use in order to have a rational business discussion about an expenditure.
3. Educate managers early on about how to estimate impact of investments and actions on the bottom line. Particularly in Japan, few managers have ever been taught how to do this, or asked to think in such terms. Many managers will likely need support and practice. Start early before employees are in leadership positions. Any employee who is not capable of this is not ready for any kind of management position.
4. Reward managers for the behavior of expenditure with reasonable business risk, about which both the manager and the funder agree, even if the project doesn't pan out. If you reward managers only for successful results and not for successful behaviors of taking

reasonable business risk regularly, your managers will avoid all
risk—which serves the business in no positive way whatsoever. It's
worse if you penalize managers for taking on good ideas that don't
work out.

5. Give an award for the best idea that didn't work, to make it clear
that in your company's culture, you value taking reasonable business risk as a behavior, and not just success.

So, the next time a manager asks for a resource, have them do a business case sprint if you are concerned that the decision will be delayed
as different parties hem and haw over the expenditure. Make a decision
rapidly using this method.

That speed, whether the decision is positive or negative, accelerates
growth in the business. If the decision is positive, great! You're moving
on a business growth opportunity fast. If it is negative, great! You've
avoided an expenditure that doesn't make sense so that managers can
move on to other better ideas, as opposed to waiting for movement on
one that may be destined for rejection or simply oblivion. Make the business case sprint an inherent part of your business.

Personal Growth Sprint

In my experience, it is difficult for a person to focus on improving more
than two capabilities at one time. That does not mean that, during the
course of a year or more, a manager cannot improve several capabilities;
but in the process of improvement it is best to focus on only one or two
at a time. Short bursts of focusing on one or two areas of improvement
is the most effective path to self-improvement, even for an agenda which
may contain multiple areas of improvement during the course of a year.

I have had a love for learning foreign languages since I was a teenager, and I now speak Japanese and French fluently, but can also speak
a smattering of Italian, German, and Mandarin Chinese. I have found that
one of the keys to learning a language is immediate application of whatever you learn. For example, if you learn the word for, say, "attitude" in
Japan, you need to use it immediately. You can make up a sentence yourself, imagining it in the context of a conversation, or better yet, work it
into your next conversation with anyone. Is your language ability not yet

good enough for that? If you are living in Japan, and learn the word for "carrots," walk into a grocery store, go up to a clerk, and ask, "Where are the carrots?" even if you are not really shopping for any. If you do that, words, expressions, and grammar will stick because you have applied what you have learned in the context of real life. You will also achieve corollary learning around what you applied for the same reason. So for example, after asking the clerk where the carrots are, you will likely also pick up on how directions are given, the words for "aisle" and perhaps "shelf," expressions for "next to" or either types of proximity, etc. All of this learning will stick far better than memorizing vocabulary lists and grammatical expressions. I can often recall exactly when and in what context I learned a word in Japanese or French, even if it was decades ago. Learning by doing is that powerful.

In management, it is the same. For example, I was coaching a mid-level manager who was being prepared for a vice president's position. A Japanese-speaking European, he was frequently encountering resistance from Japanese managers over whom he had no authority but with whom he needed to collaborate in order to achieve his objectives. He would propose a way forward using a new method, and other managers resisted, preferring the old ways to which they were accustomed.

I taught him several techniques to work through recalcitrance, which we role played. Then I asked him to apply these immediately in the next work week, which he did. The techniques worked, he internalized them and continued to use them, and we moved on to the next area of improvement.

There are two keys to rapidity in personal growth sprints—specific behaviors and accountability. So, for example, the manager I described above was responsible for his own leadership capability improvement. However, leadership capability improvement in itself is too vague to take concrete action. We had to narrow that down to specific contexts, behaviors, and desired results. The context in this particular instance was other managers resisting better ways of achieving strategic results. The behaviors are the techniques I coached the manager in using. The desired results are the other managers changing their behaviors and the business results that behavior change achieves. Accountability means that I held the manager I was coaching accountable for applying the techniques rather than falling back into the old patterns of behavior.

There is no reason why a manager cannot achieve personal growth on his own. However, many managers will benefit greatly from the support of a coach. For example, a manager might not know how to go about achieving improvement, even though they would like to do so. I coached the manager in the example above in techniques he did not know. He may have come up with these on his own, but that might have taken a lot longer. The benefit of coaching is speed. A reduction in time to improvement can make a difference of millions of dollars to the bottom line. In addition, a manager may have trouble holding themselves accountable for the change. When you are working on your own, it is easy to slip into old patterns of behavior if there isn't someone there to catch you. A coach helps with accountability. At the same time, anyone who is going to achieve personal improvement, whether with the help of a coach or not, must be capable of holding themselves accountable. Those who cannot hold themselves accountable will achieve little or no improvement, whether a coach supports them or not. As discussed previously, all leaders should serve as coach to their staff. However, at times, a business can benefit greatly from using skilled external coaches.

When applying learning in a real context is not available, the next best option is role playing. Whether a manager is learning to coach their own staff, or handle a complex sale negotiation with a key customer, there is no better educational tool than role playing. Companies whose sales teams regularly practice role playing outperform competitors whose sales teams do not. In one my client companies, I taught a group of sales managers how to carry out role plays with their staff. Most of the managers scheduled weekly or biweekly role play sessions with their teams. Some scheduled them monthly or less frequently. The frequent role playing teams significantly outperformed their infrequent role playing colleagues, even teams with sales people who had been top performers prior!

The keys to personal growth sprints are as follows:

1. Focus on one or two areas of improvement at a time.
2. Immediately apply in real context what is learned.
3. If real context is not available, the next best option is role playing, even for managers and executive-level people.

4. Self-accountability, and if a manager has trouble with that, get some support to hold the manager accountable. A manager may even ask for help from a trusted colleague or boss.
5. Consider support from external coaches. A coach can accelerate time to improvement.
6. All managers with staff should also serve as coach.

You can find additional resources on the topics discussed in this chapter and more at *www.relansa.co.jp.*

CHAPTER 9

Perpetual Leadership Bench

M any CEOs in Japan, of both Japanese and non-Japanese companies, complain about a dearth of leadership bench in their organization, despite a plethora of managers with the right titles. However, most often the objection to internal candidates for leadership is a lack of confidence in a candidate's willingness or ability to help in the execution of a significant organizational change that the CEO is leading. If this assessment is accurate, then promoting a manager into such a position only creates or enlarges refraction in the organization.

For example, the CEO of one company once told me, "The problem is I don't think any of my senior executives are ready for a COO position. Each of them is wedded to an old way of doing things, and has resisted change up to now. In the case of my sales director, he feels committed to our traditional customers and views selling into new markets with new business models as a betrayal. I cannot have such thinking among the senior leadership if we are to succeed with our new strategy."

In previous chapters, I have discussed how refraction layers and the associated dearth of leadership bench is often a result of years of seniority-based promotion and lifetime employment practices. Removing these practices helps improve organizational capabilities in general, including leadership capability. Yet it is also possible to accelerate cultivation of leadership bench through other practices. An ample pool of leadership candidates is one of the best ways to prevent refraction layers from forming in the first place.

Leadership may start at the top, but cultivating new leaders starts at the bottom. The key to perpetual leadership bench is building leadership cultivation into routine daily business practice, as opposed to leadership development programs and courses, and that starts with developing a mentor culture.

Mentor Culture

Are you a leader now? Are you good at leadership? Are you passionate about leadership and find leading rewarding? What had the greatest impact on you in developing your own leadership capability and style? I often ask this last question when talking with talented and successful CEOs. I have never heard any leader say that it was a leadership training course that had the most impact on them.

In fact, most leaders whom I ask about any leadership training they may have received rarely remember the content. Instead, they talk fondly about a particular person who helped them learn. Sometimes it was a former boss, and other times simply another leader with whom they had a trusting relationship. In all cases, it is someone who served as a mentor, teacher, and model to emulate. Most of the time the mentor relationship is informal—the mentor and the mentored simply chose each other through natural affinity. Other times, the mentor and mentored were matched in a formal program of some type. The mentored learn from the mentor while actually leading themselves—whether a small team or a team of a few people, a whole division, or a whole company. The learning occurs *in vivo*. The most successful leaders learn from other leaders while leading others themselves.

The best way to ensure an adequate leadership bench inside your company is to develop a mentor culture inside your company. You can institutionalize leadership development through specific practices of current managers at all levels who lead any number of staff. Leadership development should be something that is ongoing all the time as part of daily work, not just reserved for a select set of candidates and specific times for seminars and workshops.

Poet Maya Angelou once observed that you train animals, but people you educate. What is the difference? Training tends to focus on facts and mechanical, repetitive processes. A trainee is told the right answer to a specific question, asked to memorize it and regurgitate it when asked. Training can be effective when you want a specific response to predictable scenarios, or little variance in a repetitive process. For example, you can train people how to develop a sales forecast, how to respond to a customer who asks for a discount, how to analyze a report of results, and so on. Training is good for people you don't really want to think too hard, or require to think too hard. There are many managers who rely on minions of these kinds of people, although I question how optimal this may be.

Education is principle-based. People learn not what the right answers are, but how to ask the right questions. Education is a personal exploration of oneself which can be led by an educator, good coach, or mentor. Learning is at its most effective when it is experiential and active, as opposed to absorbing knowledge in a classroom or seminar room setting.

What separates the good leader from the good manager is the ability to do what is right as opposed to what is expedient, particularly when there is a significant and immediate penalty for doing what is right with any possibility of a return in the future being unclear. For example, a client of mine, the European CEO of a European subsidiary in Japan who had recently come into the position, discovered that his predecessor, a Japanese CEO, had been using the company bank account to support his own personal, lavish lifestyle. The Japanese CEO was nearing retirement. The company had intended to keep him on for another year to aid in transitioning to the new CEO, prior to discovering the improprieties. Instead, the new CEO forced his predecessor to resign. The problem remained what to say to customers about this and how to handle remaining staff who may have been complicit in the improper practices.

The new CEO consulted with the head office, and chose a course of action. Some weeks later he confided to me, "I think we made the wrong decision, and am not sure what to do."

The CEO explained, "We decided to tell our customers that the transition had already been moved up so my predecessor can take early retirement, and then talk about future business. Many of our customers didn't buy this story. Some key customers even halted orders. Some customers think that I pushed the former CEO out for personal reasons or that the company was discriminating against him because of his age, none of which is the case. What should I say to our customers?"

The dilemma for the CEO was that pursuing the current course of action could ultimately result in placating customers, but left the customers suspicious of his character and company values. Telling the truth about what happened, the CEO felt, would cause customers to flee altogether. And then, this CEO is worried about his own career. The Japan office had been performing poorly compared to other operations in the world. He felt that he could turn it around. The last thing he wanted to do was to return to head office after a year or more of work, not only having failed but perhaps even overseeing a withdrawal from the Japan market! What would you do?

A leadership training course cannot prepare a leader for this kind of dilemma. The options seem to be between bad and worse, both for the business and for the manager personally. How would you handle this situation? What principles do you think are at play here? What is the best course of action?

A second dilemma also remains. What to do about the senior sales executives, who had been at least complicit in the practices of the former

CEO, although to what degree is not known. The new CEO had already removed many of the former staff who had been tainted, but was reluctant to remove the sales people.

The new CEO explained, "If I could, I would remove the sales people, but who do I replace them with? I cannot handle sales here on my own. We had been trying to hire new sales managers before this crisis, and were having no success finding qualified candidates as it was. I feel I need to keep these sales managers, or otherwise shut down the business."

What would you do? What principles are at work here? What is right as opposed to expedient? Would you have the courage to do what you think is right?

Leadership mettle is determined in these types of situations. The higher up you go in an organization, the more complex these types of dilemmas become and the harder to resolve

Now imagine if this CEO had a coach, a mentor, or confidant with whom to discuss the issues he is trying to resolve. A coach might ask some provocative questions to help the CEO work through the issues. Some examples are below:

Do you think all your customers are completely unaware of the CEO's behavior? Don't you think many already may suspect it, if not knowing for sure? Do you think some may have been complicit? In this case, do you think whitewashing the issue will inspire confidence to continue business with your company?

Will your customers believe that you are committed to your values and serious about not tolerating corruption if sales people who were involved remain in your company? Do you really believe that any single person in your company is irreplaceable? If we worked on an interim solution while you were seeking new staff, don't you think we could find one together? What influence do you think current staff would have on new-hires to the company?

Support from a mentor or coach while a leader is facing real leadership issues is a powerful tool for learning. While the example above may be exceptional, and also at a relatively high level of management, the same still holds for other issues at all management levels. Some examples are below:

- How best to hold staff accountable for behaviors and results
- How to encourage open discussion and debate to elicit new ideas to improve the business when staff are typically passive

- How to help staff continuously improve
- How to help staff succeed in transitioning during a significant change in the business
- How to think strategically as opposed to operationally

I have written previously that every manager is or should be a coach to their staff. Leadership as a capability cannot be developed in a single session of training. It is a capability that must be cultivated over time in practice and by way of application. It is best learned by being a follower of a superb leader and by closely observing them. Education by way of a role model works. A manager is also in an ideal position to cultivate leadership capability in their subordinates, as they are present, and can meet regularly for the purpose of educating and coaching. The best part of this approach is that the manager is not taking time out to coach staff. Rather, this is "time in," because it helps business objectives for which both the staff person and the manager are responsible.

I recommend to all my clients to institute a practice for all managers of regularly coaching and mentoring staff. Some managers will need support in learning how to be a coach. If, in your organization, you have not institutionalized managers coaching staff before, start at the top. If you are a CEO, start by coaching and mentoring your leadership team. Once you and they feel comfortable with the process and believe it is valuable, encourage your leadership team to do the same with their staff. You serve as the model that they seek to emulate. Continue the process on down through the organization. Once the behaviors of mentoring and coaching become common and people find these valuable, you will have developed a mentor culture inside your business. While it may take time, this is the best way to ensure competent leadership bench at all levels of the organization in the long-run, and you will also find that managers at all levels of the organization are more capable than before. In the end, that will impact business results, innovation, and ability to master change. A mentor culture is key to all of these.

Encourage Failure

Leaders have the right to fail. It goes with the job. You make your decision and then you live with the consequences. We all love success, and success is always the goal. Yet the path to success is inevitably littered with failures. At the same time, success is never a permanent state. It is always ephemeral. A leader must again and again be able to handle and recover from further failures to achieve a new level of success. Managers who are squeamish about failure cannot become good leaders. For example, a Japanese senior-level manager in charge of product development held his staff back from talking with customers about new product concepts as a way to perform early market validation before investing time, people, and money into a development project. His reasoning was, "What if we failed to ultimately develop the product? Our customers would not trust us any longer!"

As a result, the team continued to tinker away on mundane technical enhancements to current products, many of which achieved little traction in the market, or otherwise devoted their time to specific product development projects for a customer requested by a sales team. These products were often one-shot deals, and despite platitudes about how the product might be sold to other customers, this rarely happened, and the company's warehouse still remains full of leftover stock from these one-shot projects.

Rather than being a spearhead of innovation for the company, the product development team lumbered along safely, barely producing enough value to justify its existence. The missed business opportunities are staggering. After years of working in this way, the company is in serious danger of obsolescence within the next ten years. All because a single manager, albeit one critically placed, is afraid to fail, imagining unlikely scenarios with the worst possible consequences attached, while the real irreparable damage to the company is due to his avoidance of failure—damage that could ultimately lead to the failure of the business if he is left unchecked.

This is not entirely the manager's fault. For decades the company's leadership had a practice of only rewarding success, and penalizing people for any failure. Penalties could occur in the form of being sidelined from promotion, cut bonuses, and sometimes public ridicule by the company CEO. These practices are not altogether uncommon in many companies in Japan, both domestic and foreign. If you are leading an organization whose reins have been passed to you, you inherit the culture created by those ahead of you either through deliberate action or neglect. It is up to you either to build upon or to break that culture and remake it if need be.

You create culture by rewarding behaviors that you value. So, for example, creating an award for "the best idea that did not work" may seem an anathema to people, but the idea is to encourage and recognize behavior of coming up with new ideas, which is critical if you are ever to succeed at all, not just with success—or worse—punishing people for testing new ideas that failed! What can you do in your business to change attitudes toward failure?

Pride and Arrogance are not the Same Thing: The Real Role of Humility

Humility is often valued in Japan, as it is in many countries. However, in Japan the value of humility tends toward the extreme compared to elsewhere. It can be considered rude to talk about one's successes and achievements. If someone pays you or someone in your family a compliment, the response is not "Thank you," but rather "No, it's not true! I really lack talent/ability/looks/smartness!" It is not unusual for a Japanese person to say about themselves, "I am ordinary," as if it were a badge of honor. To do otherwise is considered arrogant.

As a result, people can often strive to be "ordinary," and even to shun excellence. Don't get me wrong, most people will strive to do a very good job, or at least one that is not obviously inferior. However, sometimes that striving for excellence in Japan is tempered by a desire not to stand out too far compared with others. We want our mid-level managers to strive for excellence, as opposed to simple mediocrity of a high standard.

The problem is frequent confusion between pride and arrogance. Sometimes, these concepts are used interchangeably in Japan. Yet pride and arrogance are not the same thing.

Pride is confidence in your ability to provide value to others, satisfaction in having done so in the past, and letting people know what you contribute out of a desire to provide value for them. Arrogance is a belief that you have nothing left to learn from others. Such a belief results in eventually contributing no value to the organization, and also to oneself.

The role of humility is to keep arrogance in check—to remind oneself constantly, no matter what level of success one may achieve, that there is always something new to be learned and value to contribute to the world. Unfortunately, humility can also keep pride in check when a person cannot distinguish between pride and arrogance, leading to unfulfilled potential, squandered value, and a lost contribution to the world.

Arrogance is deadly. However, there is absolutely nothing wrong with pride. We all have something of value to offer to the world, and it is incumbent upon each of us to let others know! If not, the world loses out and is not as good a place as it could have been.

Pride is not just a feeling one keeps to oneself. It must be expressed, shouted, trumpeted, and communicated to all, without hesitation or shame. Pride allows us to help others make the world a better place. I believe every human being on the face of the planet has something of value to offer to the world, whether they choose to do so or not. It is in our nature as human beings to create value for others.

No matter who you are, express your pride. If you are a leader of any type, talk with your people about the difference between pride and arrogance. Encourage pride, and the open expression of pride. Praise people for sharing successes and achievements. Encourage constant learning. End the misuse of humility in keeping pride in check. Make this your culture so that your mid-level managers practice the same with their staff.

From Refraction Layer to Hunger for Success

Changing the mindset of people in an organization requires boldness and decisive action on the part of the leader. It is an endeavor that is inherently disruptive. Some will be enthusiastic about change, others will put up resistance both passive and active, and many will simply be indifferent and hold back until they see the winds of change—and judge whether or not you are committed enough to hold the managers to whom they report accountable for delivering the change. You must demonstrate that commitment through consistent action or you will lose credibility with the majority of staff in the organization.

In this book, I have discussed the means for eliminating refraction layers and achieving rapid change in your organization. Let me distill these into seven principles.

Steve's Seven Principles for Eliminating Refraction Layers and Achieving Rapid Change

1. People around the world are more similar than dissimilar. Build on our commonality as opposed to being derailed by what sets us apart.
2. The most important attribute of a mid-level manager is growth-orientation. Everything else can be learned, hired, or outsourced.

3. Overprotection of labor leads to organization brittleness. Protect and promote your stars.
4. Constructive disharmony is a good thing, as opposed to harmony for harmony's sake.
5. Performance deficits have three causes, of which training addresses only one. Understand the cause before applying a solution.
6. Sprint frequently for faster improvement.
7. Mentor culture creates leadership bench.

Have a look at these as a quick reference to what you have read. Now pick two of them, and begin to think of what actions you can take now.

There is a tendency among leaders in Japan, particularly expat CEOs who may have little experience in Japan, to believe they must tread lightly here for fear of violating some unwritten rules of Japanese culture. As we discussed, these largely do not exist, although you may find your Japanese staff, customers, and suppliers cautioning you about these nebulous rules as self-appointed experts whenever you propose a change which they find threatening. The same CEO who in any other country would push on anyway making their own strategic decisions frequently hesitates in Japan.

I have observed what I call "change fatigue" in Japan. An expat CEO comes in with bold ideas for improving the business, only to encounter passive and active resistance at every turn. They become browbeaten, exhausted, and cynical, and ultimately give up. "Why work so hard only to suffer with little substantial progress?", they may reason. It is easier to ride out their term, achieving acceptable results for the head office, and leave the rest for their successor as they move on to another assignment. Most expat CEO positions last only three to five years, so the wait is rarely long.

Don't allow yourself to be browbeaten as you begin to take action described in this book. For in every case of a leader taking action to achieve a change, it is not the browbeating from others that ultimately halts them. Rather, it is self-browbeating that pushes them off the rails. If you are browbeating yourself now, stop it. If you are preparing to enact a change, don't allow yourself to be beaten down. Remember, most people in your organization are open to change. It is more frequently the recalcitrance of a group of mid-level managers that is imposed on all.

Decisions of strategic import always imply change of some type. There will always be people who are threatened by that change, and they will react. However, rather than admitting fear or seeking support, they will try to reason with you as to why your decision is a poor one.

Poor decision or not, the decision is yours to make. Leaders have the right to make mistakes as they are the ones who are held accountable for results. Strategic decisions must be taken by the leader, and by the leader alone. Make your own decisions, live by the consequences, learn from the mistakes, and never cease striving for improvement.

There is a difference between playing to win as opposed to playing not to lose. The former is motivated by a hunger for victory and success, whereas the latter is striving to avoid the pain of defeat. In the same way, a sports team can never become champions by constantly playing a defensive game, and an individual cannot learn or become successful by always avoiding failure, a business cannot grow when its managers are driven by fear of getting things wrong as opposed to the satisfaction from getting things right. Create this mindset from top to bottom in your organization and you will have eliminated the refraction layer.

You can find additional resources on the topics discussed in this chapter and more at *www.relansa.co.jp.*

Index